PreK-2

Scott Fore

ELL   ion
Hanc

PEARSON
Scott
Foresman

Editorial Offices: Glenview, Illinois • Parsippany, New Jersey • New York, New York
Sales Offices: Boston, Massachusetts • Duluth, Georgia • Glenview, Illinois
Coppell, Texas • Sacramento, California • Mesa, Arizona

ISBN: 0-328-14555-6

5 6 7 8 9 10 V031 14 13 12 11 10 09 08 07

Contents

Overview: Support for English Language Learners

This **ELL and Transition Handbook** provides practical tips and professional development for teachers who are supporting the literacy development of young English language learners. The instructional strategies for English language learners that are embedded in *Scott Foresman Reading Street* are explained in detail in this Handbook. Additional articles and lessons will help teachers customize support for English language learners in reading, writing, listening, and speaking at all levels of English proficiency.

E L L How to Use the ELL and Transition Handbook

Introduction Refresh your awareness of English language learners in the United States by reading this brief article.

Part One: English Language Learning and Literacy Expand your repertoire of successful strategies for developing English literacy skills in children at all levels of English proficiency.

Lay the groundwork by reading:

• Jim Cummins on the Three Pillars of English language learning

• Georgia Earnest García on best practices for literacy

• Lily Wong Fillmore on preparing English learners for assessment

Learn effective strategies through these research-based articles and accompanying reproducible teaching and assessment tools:

• Welcoming Newcomers

• Sheltering Instruction

• What Reading Teachers Should Know About Language

• Vocabulary Strategies

• Effective Writing Instruction

• Cultural Affirmation and Family Involvement

• Helping the Helpers (aides, tutors, and classroom volunteers)

• English Language Learners and Assessment

Part Two: Grammar Instruction for English Language Learners Choose lessons and practice pages from this section to supplement regular grammar instruction. These Grammar Transition Lessons and Practice Pages, designed especially for young English language learners, will help children "unlock" the English language, build sentences, and use nouns, verbs, adjectives, adverbs, and pronouns correctly, extending their language knowledge.

Part Three: Phonics Instruction for English Language Learners Address children's needs by teaching or reinforcing print awareness and alphabet skills, and tackle the challenging letter-sound correspondences that pose difficulties for English language learners as emergent readers. Choose the appropriate Phonics Transition Lessons and Practice Pages to provide instruction on consonant sounds and blends, varying English vowel sounds, and other phonics challenges. Teach word study skills involving word endings, contractions, prefixes, suffixes, compound words, cognates, and other vocabulary builders.

Professional Resources and the **Index** are helpful reference tools.

Introduction:
English Language Learners

Teachers and schools across the United States are welcoming increasing numbers of English language learners (ELLs) into their classrooms. English learners make up the fastest growing K–12 student population in the United States. Since the 1989–1990 school year, the population of English learners in U.S. public schools has nearly doubled (Padolsky, 2005). The current enrollment of English language learners is about 5.5 million, and it is expected that this student population will continue to grow over the next several decades (Collier and Thomas, 2002; Leos, 2004).

While Spanish is the home language of the greatest number of English learners in U.S. schools, more than 400 different languages are spoken in schools across the country (Kindler, 2002). Most states have experienced an influx of ELL enrollment. The states with the largest student populations of English learners include California, Texas, New York, Florida, Illinois, and Arizona (Padolsky, 2005). Nearly every educator in all fifty states has become more aware of the needs of English learners.

In the current legislative climate, English language learners are expected to participate in yearly high-stakes tests. Research has consistently shown that ELL children usually require at least five years, on average, to catch up to native-speaker norms in academic language proficiency (Cummins, 1981). Nevertheless, many English learners must take the tests whether or not they have developed academic language proficiency in English.

While English language learners share many characteristics with other students, they need types of support and scaffolding that are specific to them. They represent a highly diverse population. They come from many home language backgrounds and cultures. They have a wide range of prior educational and literacy experiences in their home languages. They come to school with varying levels of English language proficiency and experience with mainstream U.S. culture.

Teachers need support to identify and respond appropriately to the varying needs of English learners in their classrooms. They need to know how to help these children develop fluency as readers, writers, listeners, and speakers of academic English at the same time that the children are required to learn grade-level content-area concepts. Yet many teachers have not had opportunities to receive specialized training. They feel unprepared to help English learners excel.

This Handbook is designed to help teachers, whether they have one English learner in the classroom or many. It offers strategies and activities to help teachers scaffold and support their instruction so that all English learners can learn in ways that are comprehensible and meaningful, and in ways that promote the academic success and achievement of all students.

References

Collier, V., and W. Thomas, 2002. *A National Study of School Effectiveness for Language Minority Students' Long-Term Academic Achievement.* Santa Cruz, CA, and Washington, DC: Center for Research on Education, Diversity & Excellence. http://www.crede.org/research/llaa/1.1_es.html

Cummins, J., 1981. The Role of Primary Language Development in Promoting Educational Success for Language Minority Students. In *Schooling and Language Minority Students: A Theoretical Framework.* Sacramento, CA: California Department of Education.

Kindler, A. L., 2002. *Survey of the States' Limited English Proficient Students and Available Programs and Services: 2001–2002 Summary Report.* Washington, DC: U.S. Office of English Language Acquisition.

Leos, K., 2004. *No Child Left Behind.* Paper presented at the annual conference of the National Association for Bilingual Education, Albuquerque, New Mexico.

National Center for Education Statistics, 2002. *Public Elementary/Secondary School Universe Survey 2001–2002* and *Local Education Agency Universe Survey 2001–2002.* Washington, DC: U.S. Department of Education Institute for Education Sciences.

Padolsky, D., 2005. *How Many School-Aged English Language Learners (ELLs) Are There in the U.S.?* Washington, DC: National Clearinghouse for English Language Acquisition (NCELA). http://www.ncela.gwu.edu/expert/faq/01leps.html

Part 1
English Language Learning and Literacy

Contents

The Three Pillars of English Language Learning

Dr. Jim Cummins, the University of Toronto

In order to understand how English learners develop second-language literacy and reading comprehension, we must distinguish between three different aspects of language proficiency:

Conversational fluency This dimension of proficiency represents the ability to carry on a conversation in face-to-face situations. Most native speakers of English have developed conversational fluency by age 5. This fluency involves use of high-frequency words and simple grammatical constructions. English learners generally develop fluency in conversational English within a year or two of intensive exposure to the language in school or in their neighborhood environments.

Discrete language skills These skills reflect specific phonological, literacy, and grammatical knowledge that students can acquire in two ways—through direct instruction and through immersion in a literacy-rich and language-rich environment in home or in school. The discrete language skills acquired early include:

- knowledge of the letters of the alphabet
- knowledge of the sounds represented by individual letters and combinations of letters
- the ability to decode written words

Children can learn these specific language skills concurrently with their development of basic English vocabulary and conversational fluency.

Academic language proficiency This dimension of proficiency includes knowledge of the less frequent vocabulary of English as well as the ability to interpret and produce increasingly complex written language. As students progress through the grades, they encounter:

- far more low-frequency words, primarily from Greek and Latin sources
- complex syntax (for example, sentences in passive voice)
- abstract expressions

Acquiring academic language is challenging. Schools spend at least 12 years trying to teach all students the complex language associated with academic success. It is hardly surprising that research has repeatedly shown that English language learners, on average, require *at least* 5 years of exposure to academic English to catch up to native-speaker norms.

Effective instruction for English language learners is built on three fundamental pillars.

Activate Prior Knowledge/ Build Background

No learner is a blank slate. Each person's prior experience provides the foundation for interpreting new information. In reading, we construct meaning by bringing our prior knowledge of language and of the world to the text. The more we already know about the topic in the text, the more of the text we can understand. Our prior knowledge enables us to make inferences about the meaning of words and expressions that we may not have come across before. Furthermore, the more of the text we understand, the more new knowledge we can acquire. This expands our knowledge base (what cognitive psychologists call *schemata,* or underlying patterns of concepts). Such comprehension, in turn, enables us to understand even more concepts and vocabulary.

It is important to *activate* students' prior knowledge because students may not realize what they know about a particular topic or issue. Their knowledge may not facilitate learning unless that knowledge is brought to consciousness.

Teachers can use a variety of strategies to activate students' prior knowledge:	
Brainstorming/Discussion	Visual stimuli
Direct experience	Student writing
Dramatization	Drawing

When students don't already have knowledge about a topic, it is important to help them acquire that knowledge. For example, in order to comprehend texts such as *The Midnight Ride of Paul Revere,* students need to have background knowledge about the origin of the United States.

Access Content

How can teachers make complex academic English comprehensible for students who are still in the process of learning English?

We can *scaffold* students' learning by modifying the input itself. Here are a variety of ways of modifying the presentation of academic content to students so that they can more effectively gain access to the meaning.

Using Visuals Visuals enable students to "see" the basic concepts we are trying to teach much more effectively than if we rely only on words. Among the visuals we can use are:

- *pictures/diagrams*
- *vocabulary cards*
- *real objects*
- *graphic organizers*
- *maps*

Dramatization/Acting Out For beginning English learners, *Total Physical Response*, in which they follow commands such as "Turn around," can be highly effective. The meanings of words can be demonstrated through *gestures* and *pantomime.*

Language Clarification This category of teaching methods includes language-oriented activities that clarify the meaning of new words and concepts. *Use of dictionaries*, either bilingual or English-only, is still the most direct method of getting access to meaning.

Making Personal and Cultural Connections We should constantly search for ways to link academic content with what students already know or what is familiar to them from their family or cultural experiences. This not only validates children's sense of identity, but it also makes the learning more meaningful.

Extend Language

A systematic exploration of language is essential if students are to develop a curiosity about language and deepen their understanding of how words work. Students should become *language detectives* who investigate the mysteries of language and how it has been used throughout history to shape and change society.

Students also can explore the building blocks of language. A large percentage of the less frequently heard academic vocabulary of English derives from Latin and Greek roots. Word formation follows predictable patterns. These patterns are very similar in English and Spanish.

When students know rules or conventions of how words are formed, it gives them an edge in extending vocabulary. It helps them figure out the meanings of words and how to form different parts of speech from words. The exploration of language can focus on meaning, form, or use:

Focus on meaning Categories that can be explored within a focus on meaning include:

- *home language equivalents or cognates*
- *synonyms, antonyms, and homonyms*
- *meanings of prefixes, roots, and suffixes*

Focus on form Categories that can be explored within a focus on form include:

- *word families*
- *grammatical patterns*
- *words with same prefixes, roots, or suffixes*

Focus on use Categories that can be explored within a focus on use include:

- *general uses*
- *idioms*
- *metaphorical use*
- *proverbs*
- *advertisements*
- *puns and jokes*

The Three Pillars

- Activate Prior Knowledge/ Build Background
- Access Content
- Extend Language

establish a solid structure for the effective instruction of English language learners.

English Language Learners and Literacy: Best Practices

Dr. Georgia Earnest García, the University of Illinois at Urbana-Champaign

Like other children, English language learners come to school with much oral language knowledge and experience. Their knowledge and experience in languages other than English provide skills and world knowledge that teachers can build on.

Making literacy instruction comprehensible to English language learners is essential. Many of the teaching strategies developed for children who are proficient in English can be adapted for English learners, and many strategies from an English as a Second Language curriculum are also useful in "mainstream" reading education.

Building on Children's Knowledge

It is vital to learn about each student's literacy development and proficiency in the home language. School personnel should ask parents:

- How many years of school instruction has the child received in the home language?
- Can the child read and write in that language?
- Can the child read in any other language?

Students can transfer aspects of home-language literacy to their English literacy development, such as phonological awareness and reading (or listening) comprehension strategies. If they already know key concepts and vocabulary in their home languages, then they can transfer that knowledge to English. For the vocabulary concepts they already know in their home languages, they only need to learn the English labels.

A teacher need not speak each student's home language to encourage English language learners to work together and benefit from one another's knowledge. Students can communicate in their home languages and English, building the content knowledge, confidence, and English skills that they need to participate fully in learning.

Devising activities in which students who share home languages can work together also allows a school to pool resources, such as bilingual dictionaries and other books, as well as home-language tutors or aides. A goal of home-language support is to help students who have skills in a first language to access this knowledge and use it to improve both their literacy and their knowledge in English.

Sheltering Instruction in English

Often, beginning English language learners may not understand what their classroom teachers say or read aloud in English. These students benefit when teachers shelter, or make comprehensible, their literacy instruction.

Sheltered instructional techniques include using:

- consistent, simplified, clearly enunciated, and slower-paced oral language to explain literacy concepts or activities
- gestures, photos, illustrations, drawings, real objects, dramatization, and/or physical action to illustrate important concepts and vocabulary
- activities that integrate reading, writing, listening, and speaking, so students see, hear, read, and write new vocabulary, sentence structures, and content

When it is clear from students' actions and responses that they understand what is being said, teachers can vary their strategies. As students' comprehension expands, teachers can gradually curtail their use of adapted oral language and of gestures, illustrations, and dramatizations.

Adapting Literacy Activities

Teachers can use many instructional activities developed for native English speakers with English language learners. For example, teacher read-alouds, shared reading, and paired reading can allow an English learner to follow the text during a reading. Such techniques greatly improve students' learning skills and comprehension.

Similarly, interactive journal writing, in which the teacher and student take turns writing entries, allows students to explore topics and ask questions. It also allows teachers to engage in ongoing authentic assessment of student proficiency and to pinpoint areas of misunderstanding.

Small group instruction and discussion also are helpful. Beginning English language learners benefit from the repeated readings of predictable texts with illustrations, especially when the teacher has provided a brief preview of each text to introduce the topic of the story and preview new vocabulary.

Repeated reading aloud of such predictable, patterned, illustrated texts provides English language learners with multiple opportunities to match the text they read with the words they hear. When students participate in shared reading and echo the spoken text or read the words aloud chorally, anxiety about pronunciation or decoding errors is reduced. When teachers choose texts that are culturally familiar and ask English language learners personal questions related to the text, the result is a lower-risk learning environment and an increased opportunity for students to make accurate inferences.

It is important for teachers to realize that beginning English language learners often do not recognize the meanings of English words as they decode them. Many words that typically are included in beginning reading instruction for native English speakers may not be part of the oral vocabulary of English language learners. For this reason, decoding instruction must be combined with vocabulary and comprehension instruction so that English language learners understand the goal of reading—comprehension.

Examples of Teaching Strategies

Before students read, use graphic organizers to map a concept from the selection. Let students brainstorm in pairs or small groups for words that are related to the concept. Then introduce other related words, including vocabulary from the reading. When possible, illustrate new concepts or vocabulary with drawings or photographs of the items. The graphic organizer will help orient students to the setting or context of the reading. Students will thus be familiar with the selection's subject before they begin to read.

Semantic Mapping Working with graphic organizers can help teach vocabulary and concepts in subject areas.

For example, before a reading on the subject of baby animals, have students help you to complete a semantic map showing pictures of animals and the names of baby animals. Ask them to volunteer the names for animal babies in their home language and transcribe their responses.

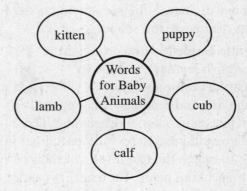

Summarizing Students can dictate what they remember from their reading to the teacher. Students can then illustrate their summaries, and label the illustrations with vocabulary from the reading.

Preparing English Language Learners for Assessment

Dr. Lily Wong Fillmore, the University of California, Berkeley

Assessment is a vital part of reading education for all children.

diagnostic evaluations

ongoing assessments during instruction

tests that measure children's learning and the effectiveness of teaching

How well do assessment techniques and instruments meet the needs of English language learners? "High-stakes" reading and content area tests, such as state tests, typically are designed and normed for proficient English speakers. How well do these assessments accommodate the developing proficiency of English learners?

Teachers look for strategies to help English learners prepare for—and perform well on—assessments, so that evaluations will reflect children's learning and inform instruction.

Active learners Teachers can help children become active rather than passive learners. Learners of English need help to prepare themselves for assessments and to perform better on both informal and formal assessments.

Helping children become active learners of English and literacy skills is central to education, and it pays dividends in assessment results for students, teachers, and schools.

Academic English How proficient must English learners become to demonstrate their mastery of language arts and reading—in English tests and other assessments? These students would need to be fully proficient in English to match the test results of their native-English-speaking peers. Yet teachers cannot declare the assessment of English language learners to be "mission impossible." Helping children improve their understanding and use of academic English is an essential way to prepare them for assessment. Here are a few strategies a teacher can use.

• Engage children in instructional conversations about reading selections and other content as often as possible, helping them hear academic English from both teacher and classmates. Find ways for the English learners to use the language as much as possible, but also recognize that children who are included in learning can achieve better grasp of English even when they are not producing polished responses.

• Draw children's attention to the features of academic language in reading selections and text materials. Help them understand it through various methods, such as these:

discussing text content in language that English learners can access more easily—that is, simpler English or, if possible, their home languages
using pictures, demonstrations, and gestures to enhance access to meaning
providing ample grade-level-appropriate discussion of content, including supportive explanations and questions for all students

Native English speakers and English learners together can learn academic language.

• Recognize that it takes years for children to master academic English, but help them make progress every step of the way.

• Teach the language used in tests and other assessments.

Assessment language The practice of "teaching to the test" is often criticized. Limiting one's teaching only to the skills and topics that figure in testing inhibits children's English learning. But helping children understand the language of tests and other assessment instruments not only helps level the playing field, but also allows children to learn more English and accurately show what they learn.

• Call children's attention to words, phrases, and constructions that often figure in test items. Words such as *both* and *not* may seem simple, but their uses in test questions prove otherwise. Help English learners understand such words and how they frame ideas.

- Teach children the logic of test questions. Use real test items or models of test items offered at many states' departments of education (or districts') Web sites. Show children, for one example, that the question "Which of the following is NOT a sentence?" entails that all of the listed choices except one <u>are</u> sentences.

- Teach children to read carefully. Native English speakers may occasionally benefit by reading test questions and then skimming test passages for answer information, but this tactic does not serve English learners well. They need to read and understand the words, ideas, and directions.

Using the Three Pillars

Think of preparing children for assessment in terms of the Three Pillars of English language learning.

- Comprehension of texts requires the **activation of prior knowledge.** English learners, like all children, have such knowledge, but they need help to see that what they know can be relevant to the text. They should bring their knowledge to bear in order to understand what they read. They also need help to use materials they read in order to **build background knowledge** for learning. Teachers support children in activating prior knowledge and building background for tests by discussing the meanings of texts and by relating what children know to new materials and ideas.

- English learners need help in **accessing the content** of texts that are presented in the language that they are learning. Teachers provide access by teaching children strategies for using context to understand and interpret texts. Examples of these strategies include:

reading texts to students, with ample discussion of meaning if students cannot yet read the texts by themselves, at least on the first go-around
guiding students to assume that the text should make sense and that meaning can be determined by figuring out what the words, phrases, and sentences mean

asking questions about meaning as it unfolds in the text
helping children recognize that some parts of many texts provide background knowledge while other parts reveal the main messages
teaching how to relate new information presented in a text to what is already known
training students to make inferences about meaning, based on the words and phrases in a text

- The texts that are read to children or that they read give them reliable access to academic English, provided that teachers call attention to the language. Teachers then can support the **extension of language** by methods such as these:

identifying interesting—not just new—phrases and commenting on them, inviting children to try using them, and providing scaffolds as needed
modeling the uses of language from texts in other activities
encouraging children to remember and keep records of words they learn from texts
reminding them when words and phrases encountered earlier show up again in different contexts

Teachers are overwhelmed by testing for accountability, but the most important testing is informal assessment that reveals how well students are learning what they need to learn; whether they understand what they read; and whether instructional activities are effective. Such assessment need not be elaborate. Monitoring participation levels can reveal who understands the materials. Asking children what they think is happening in a text reveals their comprehension. Asking children what they think words or phrases mean can show whether they are trying to make sense of text.

With the help of teachers—and their own engagement in comprehension—English learners can prepare for and improve their performance in informal and formal assessments.

Welcoming Newcomers
to the Mainstream Classroom

Students who are new to the United States or to English-language instruction are among the most challenging and rewarding students to teach.

Newcomers offer great potential to enrich the classroom experience of all students. They can share a wealth of experience and prior knowledge with their classmates.

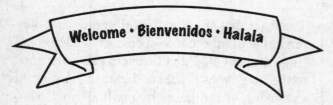

Welcome • Bienvenidos • Halala

Newcomers' levels of educational experience vary widely. Some may be fluent in conversational English and other languages and will be familiar with school environments. Others may never have attended school before. Some will be highly literate in their home languages, and some may have minimal or no literacy skills.

The teacher's first concern must be to help each child learn the basic concepts and vocabulary needed to participate in school life.

Prepare

Learn as much as possible about your newcomer students in order to tailor instruction to their individual needs. Consider drawing up a checklist:

Name_____

Home language?_____

Reads in home language? __Yes__No

Writes in home language? __Yes__No

Do family members read?__Yes__No

Is child read to at home? __Yes__No

Family can help with homework?__Yes__No

Find out from parents or other sources about educational practices in the student's home country or culture. For example, if the child is accustomed to memorizing and reciting material in a group, he or she may feel anxious about independent work or homework, particularly if the family is not able to help the child in English.

Newcomers who are acquiring English may experience identifiable stages of adjustment and adaptation.

• **A Silent Period** For a child quite new to an English-language environment, a "silent period" is normal. During this period, children chiefly watch and listen. The child may be learning classroom routine and acquiring basic vocabulary by watching and listening. Recognize that the child is learning even though he or she may not yet be speaking in class. After a time, students will gain confidence and begin to join in class activities.

• **Culture Shock** The abrupt severing of ties to anything familiar can cause newcomer students to experience stresses that may affect schoolwork. As part of the process of working through such stresses, some children may enter a short regression phase. In this phase, newcomers may prefer to spend much of their time with family or friends from the home culture and to temporarily reject the new language and culture. Help children to cope with this phase by providing extra help and attention when possible. A bilingual friend or classroom aide can help to make the environment feel more navigable to the child and can help to alleviate any feelings of anxiety or sadness.

Getting Started in the Classroom

The first days in a new classroom are important to children and their families. Before classes begin, you may wish to plan a small reception for newcomers. Invite the students' parents or other family members, and include someone who can translate. The presence of family can lessen an English learner's nervousness and introduce family members to you and to the school environment and resources.

- **Orient the newcomer to the classroom.** Have children help you to label the classroom and the objects in it with sticky notes. Pronounce the name of each item as you do, and use the word in a short sentence. "*Desk. This is your desk.*"

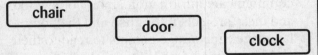

- **Demonstrate crucial skills.** Provide children with a map of the school building, with their classrooms clearly labeled. Post a seating chart where newcomers can easily see it, so that they can learn classmates' names. Go through the assigned textbooks, and help children understand what content area is covered in each book.

- **Show interest in and respect for each child's home culture.** Create opportunities for the class to learn more about the newcomer's home country and culture. Learn a few phrases in the child's home language. A cheerful greeting that includes the child's name can be used to help make the child feel welcome. Make a special effort to learn the correct pronunciation of the child's name.

- **Provide a "buddy."** A buddy system in the first weeks or months can help children navigate a new physical and social environment in ways that help them feel more secure. The buddy need not speak the same home language as the English language learner, though a buddy who does speak the same language might enable him or her to function as a peer tutor.

- **Try to provide a risk-free learning environment.** Anxiety about academic performance, especially about speaking in front of the class, can interfere significantly with a student's ability to learn. Create opportunities for children to practice speaking English without worrying about errors they may make. Accept errors in speech without comment, and model the correct phrasing.

- **Include newcomers in classroom routines.** Assign newcomers their share of regular classroom chores. Such responsibilities can help them feel they are part of the group. Children can be shown how to successfully carry out routine tasks without using or needing extensive English. Such activities, especially when performed with English-speaking partners, also can teach useful everyday vocabulary.

Teaching Strategies

Educational strategies should assist children to learn in content areas at the same time that they acquire the new language. Many commonly used teaching strategies can be adapted for English language learners. Remember that students' skills in the home language can be transferred to English learning. For this reason, encourage children to continue to speak and read in the home language. If possible, obtain the help of an English speaker who also speaks the student's home language and who can work with students to clarify key concepts.

Welcoming Newcomers to the Mainstream Classroom, continued

- **Build on students' prior knowledge.**
Newcomers often have knowledge bases that
are much greater than their skill levels in
English. Find ways to gauge children's
familiarity with the topics of upcoming
lessons. Regularly using visual aids, such as
semantic maps, K-W-L charts, or time lines,
can help you determine how much each child
already knows or needs to learn about a topic.
If you show a student a diagram of the Earth,
Sun, and Moon, for example, and ask for
words that the student can associate with the
image, you can get information about how
much the child has learned about the Solar
System.

Know	Want to know	Learned

- **Encourage children to use learning
resources.** Teach students how to use a picture
dictionary or a children's dictionary, and
encourage them to use it frequently to find the
words they need. Ask them to start their own
word banks by listing frequently used
vocabulary in a notebook. You may wish to
allow newcomers to keep their word banks in a
computer file, which would make adding new
words and alphabetizing easier. Make sure
students know where the library or media
center is and how to use it. If possible, provide
a bilingual dictionary in the classroom for
children's use.

- **Use environmental print to teach.** Put up
posters and other materials from periodicals
and magazines. If possible, provide students
with parallel texts about the same topic in
English and in the home language. Such
materials can help children make connections
between their prior knowledge in the home
language and their new English vocabulary.

- **Invite the families of newcomers to
participate in school life.** Find ways to
communicate information about homework
and class projects in English and the home
language. Encourage parents to read to their
children in the home language and, if possible,
to share stories in English. Make them aware
that literacy skills in the home language can
help students transfer those skills to English.
You might suggest titles of engaging children's
books in English or the home language that can
provide newcomers with valuable background
knowledge. Bilingual school staff or
community members may be able to help.

Good Books

1 _____
2 _____
3 _____
4 _____
5 _____

- **Build a support network.** Children may benefit in several ways from developing their English proficiency skills with the help of someone who speaks their home language. Bilingual tutors or classroom aides can clarify assignments or lesson content for language learners without disrupting the day's activities. Similarly, family members who volunteer to help in the classroom can greatly lessen students' anxiety levels. In addition, each family can support and reinforce class instruction with the child at home.

- **Help children transfer their writing skills.** For English learners who have developed any emergent writing skills in their home languages, build on these skills by occasionally having them write in both languages. Short sentences and picture labels written in a home language and English help children with writing and English acquisition. Bilingual staff members, parents, and other students may serve as valued language resources.

- **Include culturally relevant assignments.** Try to find readings for children that refer to their home cultures. Literature about the home cultures can help keep children's interest level and engagement high. If possible, have children respond to these readings orally or in writing, whether in a journal or a dictated report. If writing skills are limited, encourage children to show their understanding by talking about the stories and creating illustrations.

While it may take some time for English language learners to gain proficiency in academic English, newcomers need not feel like outsiders for very long.

Notes

Sheltering Instruction for English Language Learners

What is sheltered instruction?

Sheltered instruction is a combination of strategies for teaching academic content to English language learners at the same time that they are developing proficiency in the English language. This approach to instruction is called *sheltered* because it offers a haven, or refuge, for children who must comprehend subject matter presented in a language they are still learning. Sheltered instruction supports English learners who do not have grade-level academic vocabulary or the familiarity with the American school system that their English-speaking classmates have. It provides extended English language support that English learners receive as they learn subject-area concepts.

How does sheltered instruction help children and teachers?

Sheltered instruction offers practical, easy-to-implement strategies that teachers can use in a mainstream classroom. Many strategies will already be familiar to teachers; what is different is the emphasis sheltered instruction places on extending and scaffolding instruction about the English language. This approach allows teachers to adapt common teaching methods to teach the required content. At the same time, sheltered instruction helps English language learners find the keys they need to make sense of instruction in English about the concepts and processes they need to perform grade-level work in all subjects.

Teachers can help children build mental bridges to new concepts and learning in English by encouraging them to connect their prior knowledge—the diverse skills, experiences, language, and cultural knowledge that they bring to the classroom—to their new learning activities. Finding ways for children to draw on their home language, cultural background, and prior experience can facilitate each English learner's ability to grasp and retain abstract ideas and grade level vocabulary. Finding connections between what they are learning and what they already know in their home language can motivate children to read, write, listen, and speak in English. As comprehension and vocabulary increase, students can transfer more and more concepts from their home languages into English.

This knowledge transfer can work for teachers too. As teachers tap children's prior knowledge, the teachers will discover when they need to supply background about American events, customs, and idioms that may be new to English language learners. At the same time, they will be expanding their knowledge about English learners' backgrounds and traditions.

Some Basics

1. Use Appropriate Speech (Comprehensible Input)
   - ✓ **Enunciate.** Speak slowly and clearly, especially when introducing new content and vocabulary.
   - ✓ **Provide wait time.** English learners often need extra time to process questions in English and to formulate responses. Allowing children time to think in English demands both concentration and patience.
   - ✓ **Explain and demonstrate the meaning of complex terms.** Use activities that help children practice speaking, hearing, writing, and reading key words and phrases.

Complex term	Activities to clarify meaning
weather	Write and say: weather Write and say: hot, cold Say: The weather is hot today. (Fan yourself to show you are hot.) Then say: The weather is cold today. (Hug yourself and shiver to show you are cold.) Have volunteers repeat each sentence, with gestures. Then fan yourself and ask: What is the weather like today? (hot) Hug yourself and shiver and ask: Is the weather hot or cold today? (cold) Have partners take turns using gestures and asking and answering the questions. Start a wall chart of weather words, with pictures. Label the chart "Weather." Have children use the chart to talk about the weather each day.

✓ **Allow children to show comprehension at their level of language proficiency.** For children who are just beginning to learn English, this may mean asking questions that can be answered with "yes" or "no," by choosing one of two words as the answer ("Is ice hot or cold?"), by pointing to a picture or object ("Point to the tree."), or by following simple oral directions ("Pick up the red cube. Put the red cube next to the yellow cube.").

2. Develop Academic Concepts

✓ **Link concepts explicitly to students' prior knowledge and background.** For example, if you introduce a unit on weather, ask students to describe, illustrate, and share what they know about weather. Create and display a class chart that tells about weather in places where students have lived.

Kinds of Weather			
Puerto Rico			
☁☔	☀	🌳	
Ohio			
☁☔	☀	🌳	⛄

✓ **Use hands-on activities to build background for new information.** For example, introduce the idea of touch (The Five Senses) by having children touch objects with different textures and learn a word or words to describe how each object feels. Keep some of the objects in a "touch" box so that children can return to them on other days. Create and use wall charts, such as the one shown here, for each of the five senses.

How Does It Feel?					
pebble	smooth	**sand-paper**	rough	**water**	wet
chalk	hard	**pencil point**	sharp	**sand**	dry
cloth	soft	**tape**	sticky	**ice**	cold

✓ **Use supplementary materials.** Storybooks and picture books can clarify and support concept learning. Use picture books that show terms that are hard to explain, such as *covered wagons, rations,* or the *Pony Express.*

3. Emphasize and Develop Key Vocabulary

✓ **Repeat key words, phrases, and concepts, and have children practice using them.**

✓ **Provide feedback on children's language use.** Use gestures to indicate understanding, as well as supportive questions to prompt children to provide more details.

✓ **Make the development of proficiency in English an explicit goal in all of your teaching.** To learn academic English, children need to use it. Provide situations that challenge children to push themselves to a higher level of proficiency. Help them as needed to express something that is hard for them to put into words, and praise their efforts to expand their proficiency.

4. Connect Written and Oral Language

✓ **Say and write new vocabulary.** When teaching new words or phrases, such as idioms, write the word or phrase where everyone can see it. Say it slowly as you point to it. Have children repeat the word or phrase. Use gestures, role play, or drawings to demonstrate what the word means. Have children practice saying, reading, and writing the word or phrase in sentences.

✓ **Use word and picture cards to explain vocabulary and content.** Provide pairs of word and picture cards. Help children read and say each word as they look at the picture of the object. Have them practice naming each picture and finding the word card that matches the picture. Keep the cards available for children to work with on their own or with a partner. Have them write and illustrate the words on cards to add to their personal word files.

✓ **Have children build personal word files.** Have them write a word on one side of the card and draw a picture to represent its meaning on the other side. The files can include target words for different content areas as well as words that children find interesting or important. Have children use the cards for sorting and categorizing activities (*e.g.,* color words, animal names, weather words, math words, action words).

Word	Drawing
tent	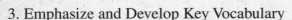

✓ **Provide letter and phoneme cards for phonics activities.** Pair English learners with native English speakers to use cards in order to build and say words that contain target sounds and spelling patterns. Give English learners extra time and support to hear, say, and practice sounds, and to build words using those sounds.

5. Use Visuals, Dramatization, and Realia (Real Things)

✓ **Use picture walks to preview text, concepts, and vocabulary—and to build background knowledge.** Before reading a story aloud or having children read it with you, "walk" through the pictures with them. Use the pictures to introduce characters and the setting and to give a simple summary of the story. For example: "This boy is Sam."

(Point to the boy. Write and say "Sam.") "Sam is playing with his dog." (Point to the dog.) "The dog is a black dog. But he has a small patch of white on his face." (Point to the patch of white.) "The dog is named Patch." (Write and say "Patch.") "Do you think Patch is a good name for this dog? Why?"

✓ **Use realia and graphic organizers.** Whenever possible, show objects and pictures that will help children understand concepts and learn how to talk about them in English. Use graphic organizers, diagrams, drawings, charts, and maps to help students conceptualize information that is abstract or difficult to understand.

✓ **Use Total Physical Response (TPR) for active learning, so that students can show comprehension through physical movement.** For example, have students hear and follow instructions: "Clap your hands for Carla." "Go to the board, and circle the noun with a red piece of chalk."

✓ **Use role-play, drama, rhymes, songs, and movement.** All children need opportunities to be active learners. For English learners, participating in a small group re-enactment of a story, for example, can allow them to show comprehension and personal responses beyond what their language abilities may allow them to express.

6. Ongoing Formal and Informal Assessment

✓ **Assess early to understand a child's language level and academic preparedness.**

✓ **Set personal goals for each child and monitor progress regularly.** For example, a child who can only respond to yes or no questions might be pushed to complete sentences, orally and in writing, with target words. A child who uses phrases might be pushed to speak and write complete sentences. A child who uses simple sentences might be pushed to add clauses to the sentences.

✓ **Provide various ways to demonstrate knowledge, including acting, singing, retelling, demonstrating, and illustrating.**

✓ **Use a variety of formal assessments such as practice tests, real tests, and both oral and written assessments.** Use multiple choice, cloze, and open response formats to help children become familiar with various assessment formats.

Sheltered instruction provides English learners with many opportunities to understand and access content area learning. Within this kind of instruction, teachers support English language learning by providing activities that integrate reading, writing, listening, and speaking. Teachers can address the range of cultural, linguistic, and literacy experiences that English learners bring to the classroom by using children's experiences and prior knowledge as topics for these activities. In this way, sheltered instruction can provide children with keys to unlock the doors to comprehension, gaining access to both content and language learning.

What Reading Teachers Should Know About Language

Why do reading teachers need to know about the structure of language?

English language learners are entering U.S. classrooms in steadily increasing numbers. The demands on teachers also are surging. To communicate effectively with these students, teachers need to know how to make their instructional talk more comprehensible. Reading teachers need to better understand their students' attempts at written and spoken language.

> "As reading teachers, we have to help children who are beginning to speak English but who are not succeeding with it in academic settings. By learning more about how English works, we discover and improve our strategies for helping children speak, listen to, read, and write English."
>
> — *Terri Murray, elementary teacher*

To improve children's literacy skills in English, teachers must understand how language works *in education.* What should we know about English and other languages? What truths about language help teachers as communicators, as guides, as evaluators, and as advocates for children?

Knowledge about the structure of languages— and particularly of English—is vital not only to linguists and ESL teachers. Reading teachers, too, can make practical, everyday use of the concepts that are posed and explored by the following questions. The answers here can provide beginnings for educators who will help English language learners achieve comprehension as readers, writers, listeners, and speakers of English.

What are the basic units of language?

Spoken language consists of units of different sizes:

Phonemes

Phonemes are the individual sounds in a word that affect meaning. The word *cat* consists of these three phonemes: /k/ /a/ /t/.

Different languages use different sets of phonemes. English language learners may not be familiar with some English phonemes and may need help recognizing and producing these sounds.

Phonemes signal different word meanings. For example, the different vowel sounds in the words *hit* and *heat* indicate that these are two different words.

TiP English language learners who cannot distinguish between the sounds /i/ and /ē/ may not initially recognize that the spoken words *hit* and *heat* are distinct words with different meanings.

Morphemes

Morphemes are the smallest units of meaning in a language. Some morphemes are **free** (or independent) units. Words such as *dog, jump,* and *happy* are free morphemes. Other morphemes are **bound** (or attached), such as inflected endings, prefixes, and suffixes:

- the noun ending *-s* in *dogs*
- the verb ending *-ed* in *jumped*
- the prefix *un-* in *unhappy*
- the adjective ending *-er* in *happier*
- the suffix *-ness* in *happiness*

These bound morphemes add meaning and, in fact, form new words.

TiP English has many kinds of bound morphemes. English learners need to learn how different bound morphemes change the meanings of words.

Words

A word consists of one or more morphemes. A word also can be defined as a meaningful group of morphemes. Native English speakers may pronounce words in ways that make it difficult for English learners to hear word boundaries. For example, in conversation, an English speaker may ask, "Did you eat?"—but pronounce it like "Jeet?"

Some languages use bound morphemes (for example, word endings) to convey the meanings of certain functional English words such as the prepositions *in, on,* and *between.* English learners may need explicit instruction in order to use these functional words correctly. On the other hand, an English word such as *in* may seem familiar to a Spanish speaker who uses the similar preposition *en.*

Phrases

A phrase is a group of words that have meaning together but do not include a subject and a predicate. Since some languages allow the subject or verb to be understood, children may believe that certain phrases in English are equivalent to sentences.

Sentences

A sentence is a meaningful group of words that includes a subject and a predicate. English language learners may understand the concept of sentences, but they may apply word order conventions from their home languages. They also may struggle with the dense sentence structures of academic English.

Discourses

Discourses include speeches, essays, and many other kinds of communication made up of sentences. One kind of discourse frequently heard in U.S. classrooms involves the teacher asking questions and students responding aloud.

TiP Depending on their home cultures, some English learners may find the question-and-response form of discourse unfamiliar.

Why do English learners need to learn about basic units of language?

It helps teachers to understand that units, such as bound and free morphemes, words, phrases, and sentences or clauses, operate differently in different languages. For example:

- In Chinese, the past tense is not expressed with verb endings, but by separate words that indicate the time of the action (similar to *yesterday* and *already*).

- In Spanish, verb endings indicate the person and number of sentence subjects, so the subject may not be stated in some sentences.

- In Arabic, related words share three-consonant roots. Speakers form related verbs, nouns, and adjectives by applying fixed patterns to these roots and sometimes adding prefixes and suffixes.

English language learners are working mentally to determine how units of English work—as they also try to understand texts and acquire content knowledge.

Depending on their home languages, English learners may already be familiar with some aspects of English, such as certain phonemes and patterns of word order. Other aspects of English will be unfamiliar and will require explicit instruction. For lessons that support challenging concepts in English grammar and phonics, see the Grammar Transition Lessons on pages 62–131 and the Phonics Transition Lessons on pages 132–203.

What is academic English?

Academic English might be described as the language of teachers, literature, textbooks, and content areas, such as science and social studies. Unlike conversational English, academic English is language of a cognitively demanding register, or range. Academic English does not depend as much upon the gestures and circumstances of speech as conversational English does.

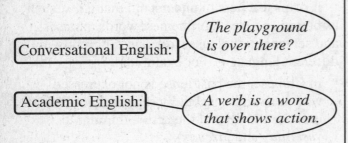

Conversational English: *The playground is over there?*

Academic English: *A verb is a word that shows action.*

Academic English includes content-area vocabulary embedded in complex grammatical structures. It features words about abstract ideas. Understanding this language requires knowledge of content, as well as experience with written materials and classroom discussions.

TiP Many English learners can carry on conversations in English with their native-English-speaking classmates. But they still struggle with reading and writing English—and even understanding their teachers in class. They have acquired social English skills used in personal communication, but they have not yet mastered the academic English used at their grade level.

How do English language learners learn vocabulary?

English language learners must learn much more than the selected vocabulary words in a lesson. They also must make sense of the other unfamiliar words in the lesson—and thousands of other words they continually encounter in school.

Knowing a word involves much more than hearing it and learning its definition. Students must learn how each word relates to its other forms. They gradually learn how it relates to other words and concepts. Knowledge of a word grows during many encounters.

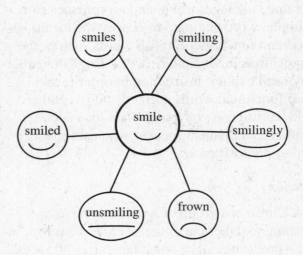

Children learn words in meaningful groups more effectively than in unrelated lists. Look for opportunities to group words in meaningful ways. For example, as children learn the word *invite,* they also can learn *invited, uninvited, invitation, inviting,* and other words in this family. As they learn the word *hippo,* they can learn other animal names, such as *rhino, buffalo,* and *elephant.*

The article "Vocabulary Strategies for Active Learners" begins on page 26.

What is "regular" to English language learners?

Proficient English speakers often take for granted irregularities in English that can puzzle younger and less fluent learners.

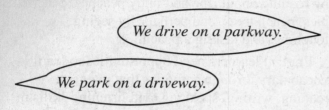

We drive on a parkway.

We park on a driveway.

For example, a child who learns the plural forms *dogs, cats,* and *turtles* may wonder why *mouses, mooses,* and *childs* meet with disapproval. A student who masters these past tense forms—*jumped, walked,* and *stopped*—may try to use *throwed, catched,* or *taked.* In both cases, the child demonstrates an awareness of English conventions, and a teacher should acknowledge this in a positive way. The teacher also should gradually help each student master the many exceptions to the rules.

short → shortness

timid → timidness

But: long → length

brave → bravery

Teachers who are aware of the principles of word formation in English can help children acquire vocabulary. English has many helpful patterns for children to learn. Savvy teachers break up the instruction into manageable chunks so that students are not overwhelmed by the many English word patterns they encounter.

What characteristics of written words challenge young English learners?

- Written English is an alphabetic language, and letters represent sounds in words. Languages such as Chinese and Japanese are not alphabetic; written symbols can represent larger parts of words than individual sounds. For students whose home languages are not alphabetic, learning the alphabetic system is an early and continuing challenge.

- The home languages of many English learners—including Spanish, Vietnamese, Hmong, Haitian Creole, and others—are alphabetic. Yet the letter-sound correspondences in these languages are different from those of English. Students can use literacy skills they may have in their home languages, but much new learning is needed to master English.

- While letter-sound correspondences in numerous languages are relatively simple, the relationships of letters to sounds in English can be complicated. In Spanish, for example, the vowel *a* has one sound. In English, *a* can represent many different sounds, as the words *cat, late, saw, Pa, marry, park,* and *dental* begin to illustrate.

- Even in related English words, the same letters can stand for different sounds. Consider *c* in the words *electric, electricity,* and *electrician.* The spelling of these words may challenge children who are learning English, but the shared *c* also indicates the meaningful link among the words.

- The challenges of written English affect not only spelling but also word recognition, comprehension of text, and confidence in language learning.

Many teaching strategies are explored in the Phonics Transition Lessons that begin on page 132 and the article "Effective Writing Instruction for English Language Learners" that begins on page 34.

Vocabulary Strategies for Active Learners

Introduction: Vocabulary Development and English Learners

The National Reading Panel (2000) has identified vocabulary development as a critical component of reading comprehension. Children who lack a well-developed vocabulary—and this includes English language learners—need extra support to extract meaning from the texts they read every day. Research shows that overall, even if they can decode words, English learners struggle with comprehension.

Learning academic vocabulary in English poses challenges for English language learners for many reasons. They are still learning the meaning of words in conversation, basic language structures, and the sounds and spelling of words.

At the same time that these children are learning English, they are being introduced to grade-level content learning, which often uses specialized vocabulary to represent abstract ideas. They may not be able to bring the necessary cultural and background knowledge to the task of unlocking the meaning of English words. For a time, this can obscure context clues that help readers figure out the meanings of new words and ideas. English learners come to school with a wide range of home language literacy, English language proficiency, and previous educational experiences. All of these factors impact their learning in English.

Teachers Support Vocabulary Learning

Teachers can use various strategies to support vocabulary development. These strategies should include helping children encounter and use the vocabulary through meaningful activities in order to understand the concepts behind the words. Children do not learn English words by hearing or seeing them and their definitions once. They need multiple exposures to words. Understanding deepens over time through gradually increased and varied experiences with the words.

For example, think of the word *peach*. A child who has never seen a peach can learn to pronounce the word or decode it in print. Yet the learner will understand the meaning more fully by reading about ripe and juicy peaches, peach pies, peach trees, and perhaps by seeing, touching, and tasting a peach.

English learners need opportunities to learn vocabulary through activities that integrate reading, writing, speaking, and listening skills in the context of meaningful literacy experiences. Language learning is an exploration, and children become "detectives" in search of meaning. Children have a curiosity about learning, and effective teachers nurture this quality through engaging and meaningful activities.

Successful vocabulary learning engages children in active learning, in ways related to meaning. English learners bring diverse experiences, knowledge, and skills to the classroom. Teachers can use what children already know to help them extract meaning from text by teaching them ways to learn and think about words.

Strategies for Exploring Words

There are many vocabulary strategies that help children explore words, extract meaning, and gain understanding. Teachers can help English learners build a foundation of vocabulary that will help them access both language and content area learning.

Related Words

Provide opportunities for English learners to learn new words by grouping words that are related to a specific theme, quality, or activity. Help children classify English words in meaningful categories.

Use word walls, graphic organizers, and concept maps to group related words and create visual references that can be used in future lessons. Teachers can help children group and relate words in different ways, depending on what children can notice and understand, as well as how children will use the vocabulary.

Color names are one example of related words that can be the focus of a lesson.

✓ Write the word *colors* at the top of a wall chart.

✓ With colored markers, make a column of squares under the heading: red, blue, yellow, green.

✓ Point to the word *colors* and tell children they are going to learn the names of colors.

✓ Point to the first square and say, "This color is red." Write *red* next to the red square and repeat it clearly as you underline it with your finger. Have children practice saying the word.

✓ Show children a familiar red object, such as a block, and say: "This is a red block. The color of this block is red. What color is this block?" (red)

Repeat this process with the other colors, making sure that children hear, say, and read each color name, and connect it to the color itself.

Over time, extend the activity by adding other colors to the wall chart and having children practice reading, writing, and saying them. Encourage children to use color words when they are describing what something looks like or are talking about their drawings. Have them add the words to personal word card files, in a section labeled "colors."

Have children create other sections in their personal word card files such as "family names," "numbers," "days and months," "weather," and "time."

Whenever you introduce a new topic or concept, take time to teach English learners words they will need to understand the lesson. Keep in mind that they may need to learn some words and phrases in the lesson—including idioms and background references—that may already be common knowledge to native speakers. Encourage native speakers to act as resources for English learners when they encounter a word, phrase, or concept that puzzles them.

Charts such as the one below can help children learn how words change form, depending on their function.

Naming Word	Describing Word	Action Word
rain	rainy	rain, rains, rained, raining
dance, dancer	dancing	dance, dances, danced, dancing
sleep, sleeper	sleepy	sleep, sleeps, slept, sleeping

Cognates

When children hear or see a word that looks or sounds similar to a word they know in their home language, encourage them to explore the connection. For example, a Russian speaker hearing the word *music* may recognize its connection to the Russian word *musika*. Many words that sound similar in two or more languages are cognates—they have the same or similar meaning in both languages. Cognates allow children to use what they know in their home language to expand their vocabulary in English. Record cognates on a wall chart and add to it during the year.

English learners also need to be warned about false cognates. The English word *soap* sounds like *sopa*, the Spanish word for *soup*, for example, but the meaning is not at all similar. You may want to develop and keep a list of false cognates on display that you add to during the year. Use it to help children create their own cognate/false cognate charts. (See pages 30–31.)

Multiple-meaning Words

Many English words have multiple meanings. Illustrating and creating examples of the ways words are used can build English learners' experiences and understanding of the multiple meanings that words may have.

Teachers can help children expand their understanding of multiple meanings by sharing sentences, definitions, and pictures that demonstrate the different meanings. For example, contrasting *The pitcher is full of water* with *The pitcher threw the ball,* with illustrations, will help English learners remember the two meanings of *pitcher.*

Illustrate the multiple meanings of words such as *pitcher* with card sets. (See page 32.) Make sets of word and sentence cards, cut them out, and have children mix the cards and match the meanings. As an extension, have children work with partners, and assign each pair a word for which they will create their own card pair to share with the class. Possibilities include *cold, duck, pen, light, sink,* and *stick.*

Academic Language

Developing academic language includes understanding "school language" and a vocabulary of technical terms and abstract meanings. Repeatedly using words and language that are common to various content areas, such as science, social studies, and math, helps English learners connect to the concepts and meanings that the words represent. Teachers can begin by targeting words that are specific to one content area, but are likely to be found in various content learning situations.

For example, create and display a wall chart of math terms and symbols that children will use over and over again, such as: *add, subtract, plus, minus, equals, fewer, less, more, place value, ones, tens, same, different.* Add to it, or create more charts, as new terms and concepts are introduced during the year.

Use word webs and charts to help children develop vocabulary they need to identify, discuss, and write about abstract concepts such as the five senses.

Sight	Touch	Taste	Smell	Hearing
shiny	hot	sweet	spicy	noisy

For academic terms related to reading itself, provide questions and graphic organizers that will prompt students to identify literary elements and/or focus on a particular strategy or skill. Have children write about concepts and then illustrate them. Alternatively, have children illustrate the concept and then help them write the word or sentence that describes the picture.

For any content area, use graphs, diagrams, or charts to illustrate academic concepts that may be hard to understand abstractly.

Home Language Activities

Teachers can use home language activities to help children reinforce their learning of the concepts and meaning of vocabulary and literacy activities. English learners can participate in a variety of activities such as discussion, telling or reading stories, listening to songs and music, hearing radio or television weather or sports reports, and interviewing family members, and then use these experiences as topics for discussion and sharing in the classroom. Children can transfer their understanding of a word or concept from their home language to English when they have experiences that illustrate the meaning.

Teachers can find ways to use the home environment as an educational resource by planning activities that involve reading, writing, listening, and speaking about children's family history, culture, and experiences.

Have children use an interview record sheet to illustrate, describe, and write about their conversation with a family member. Help children focus on words in the home language that include *dialogue/conversation/discussion; ask/inquire/interview; tell/answer/respond.* (See page 33.)

Have children use Venn diagrams to record the similarities and differences between their home country or culture and their new home or school setting that includes English. Help children focus on words in the home language that include *similarities/same/alike/compare; differences/ different/contrast; here/there.*

Technology

Teachers can use various forms of technology (computer, Internet, audio, video recording) to meet the specific and varied needs of English learners.

For example, you might choose target words and have children use computers to find images that illustrate their meaning. Have children write and illustrate the words and add them to their personal word files or dictionaries.

Word	Class or Dictionary Meaning	Home Language Word	Describe or Draw the Meaning
summer	The season between spring and fall; months of June, July, and August (Northern Hemisphere).	Spanish: *el verano* Indonesian: *Musim panas*	

Children can choose words they hear while listening to an audio book at home, try to write them, illustrate them, and bring them to school. Help them learn correct spelling and pronunciation and expand their knowledge of each word's meaning.

Creating and Adapting Strategies

The great and changing range of ideas, experiences, and needs that English language learners bring to the classroom each day call for teachers to try a variety of strategies to include these students in vocabulary instruction. Savvy teachers recognize that English learners, like all students, respond differently to instructional tactics. The truth is that students grow their own vocabularies, supported by the scaffolding that teachers provide. A great deal of reading in English, listening to selections read aloud, and conversing in English will help learners acquire thousands of words per year if they are engaged in learning, and if teachers do not give up on them. Continue the instructional strategies that work, adapt (or discontinue) the ones that are not effective, and try new approaches as needed.

References

Bear, Donald R., *et al.* (1996). *Words Their Way: Word Study for Phonics, Vocabulary, and Spelling Instruction.* Upper Saddle River, NJ: Prentice Hall.

Blachowicz, Camille L. Z., and Peter Fisher (2002). *Teaching Vocabulary in All Classrooms.* Upper Saddle River, NJ: Prentice Hall.

Center for the Improvement of Early Reading Achievement (2001). *Put Reading First: The Research Building Blocks for Teaching Children to Read.* Washington, DC: Partnership for Reading.

National Reading Panel (2000). *Teaching Children to Read: An Evidence-Based Assessment of the Scientific Research Literature on Reading and Its Implications for Reading Instruction.* Washington, DC: National Institute of Child Health and Human Development.

Vocabulary Development for Reading Success (2004), Scott Foresman Professional Development Series, Module 6. Glenview, IL: Scott Foresman.

Cognates

These related words sound similar in two or more languages. The meanings are the same.

English	Home Language
music	*música* (Spanish) *musika* (Russian)
school	*szkoła* (Polish) *escuela* (Spanish)

English	Home Language

False Cognates

These words sound similar in two or more languages.
The meanings are not the same.

English	Home Language
soap	*sopa* (Spanish)

English	Home Language

Multiple-meaning Words

pitcher	**The <u>pitcher</u> is full of water.**
pitcher	**The <u>pitcher</u> threw the ball.**
ruler	**She is the <u>ruler</u> of the country.**
ruler	**I use a <u>ruler</u> to measure things.**

Interview Record Sheet   Date _____

My name _____   Other Person's Name _____

Question	
Answer	
Question	
Answer	
Question	
Answer	
Question	
Answer	
Question	
Answer	

Effective Writing Instruction for English Language Learners

The Role of Writing in Language and Literacy Development

To provide effective writing instruction for English learners, teachers need to understand how language, literacy, and culture are related (Fillmore and Snow, 2000). When teachers understand how children's home languages and cultural backgrounds can influence how they write and how they understand writing, the teachers can find effective ways to meet the instructional needs of these children.

Research shows that children acquire language most readily when they are fully involved in all learning activities in the classroom. Classroom activities should integrate reading, writing, listening, and speaking, as these language skills develop interdependently. This approach supports English language development in the context of meaningful instructional content. That is, children will learn to write (in English) about real ideas and things.

Teachers can facilitate children's language learning and literacy development by ensuring that:

- children hear language in natural ways, in real and practical contexts—and write it in structured formats
- activities in which children participate regularly provide opportunities for listening and speaking so children can internalize the language
- opportunities for acquiring new vocabulary are always present in reading activities and environmental print, and are related to the content areas of the curriculum
- opportunities are always available for interesting conversations with English-speaking peers
- mistakes are accepted as part of learning
- children understand why they are being asked to complete various oral communication, reading, and writing tasks

English learners who are already literate, or are emergent readers and writers in their home languages, no doubt have been influenced by their backgrounds and experiences with writing genres, writing styles, and cultural discourse. By learning more about the characteristics of English learners' literacy experiences, teachers can recognize when children are transferring what they already know to their new, early literacy learning in English, and teachers can support these efforts. It is helpful to seek information about the children in sensitive ways, appropriately respecting families' privacy and regarding home languages and cultures with respect.

Such efforts to find out children's strengths and needs are worthwhile. For example, teachers who compare spelling patterns between a home language and English will better understand the efforts children make to acquire and write English words. Teachers can point out the differences and similarities so that children can learn to compare the languages and develop metalinguistic understanding about how both languages work. This will help them sort out the ways they can use language in their writing.

ENGLISH	rose
SPANISH	rosa

Young English learners also are emergent writers. For most children, the line between emergent writing and drawing (that is, art) is not a bold border. It helps children to write in both words and pictures. Experts in English language learning advise, however, that English learners who draw too often without writing any words are missing vital opportunities to practice writing in English. Encourage children to write about their pictures.

Scaffolding the Steps of the Writing Process

Writing, whether in a home language or especially in a new language, is the most difficult mode of language use to master (Collier and Ovando, 1998). Each English learner has a unique background and set of experiences with language, literacy, and culture. Children access writing instruction at varying levels of English proficiency. It is important for teachers to provide each child with challenging work that is appropriate for his or her level of English proficiency and literacy. This kind of scaffolding (Vygotsky, 1978) can provide children access to effective instruction.

By understanding the specific kinds of support English learners need at each stage of the writing process, teachers can tailor their instruction to fit individual needs. The chart below provides suggestions to help teachers do this.

	Beginner (little experience in English)	**Intermediate** (conversational but not academic English)	**Advanced** (gaining skills in academic English)
Prewrite	Allow extra time for prewriting. Use brainstorming. Have child draw or act out ideas. Map, or illustrate and label, words that the child needs.	Allow extra time for prewriting. Use brainstorming. Have child draw and label, or act out and describe, ideas. Help child learn and write the words he or she needs.	Allow extra time for prewriting. Use brainstorming, drawing, word mapping, and story mapping. Help child learn and write the words he or she needs.
Draft	Allow child to dictate, as appropriate. As skills emerge, child writes words and phrases. Accept phonetic invented spelling, but model correct spelling, capitalization, and punctuation.	Child writes words, phrases, and simple sentences. Help child turn phrases into sentences. Accept phonetic invented spelling, but show correct spelling, capitalization, and punctuation.	Child writes words, phrases, and simple sentences. Help child add details to sentences and create paragraphs. Accept phonetic invented spelling, but show correct spelling, capitalization, and punctuation.
Revise	With help, child revises work with the aid of a checklist that has visual clues about each task.	Child revises work with the aid of a checklist that has visual and written clues about each task. Help child incorporate written or oral commentary from teacher in revisions.	Child revises work with the aid of a checklist that has visual and written clues about each task—and asks for clarification. Help child incorporate written or oral comments from teacher in revisions.
Edit	Child sees teacher model how to correct errors and begins to correct errors.	Child corrects errors with help from the teacher.	Child corrects errors with help from the teacher and incorporates teacher's suggestions into writing.
Publish	Child creates final product of writing with teacher's guidance.	Child creates final product of writing with teacher's guidance.	Child creates final product of writing with teacher's guidance.

Structured Writing

Teachers can use **structured writing** to scaffold writing instruction. Structured writing aids include sentence frames and graphic organizers, which help children record and organize their ideas. Teachers need to adjust their expectations for writing to fit children's levels of English proficiency.

Writing Assignments for English Learners

There are various kinds of assignments and activities that encourage English learners to use their background knowledge and previous experiences to connect with the writing process. Establishing a daily or weekly **routine** for these assignments and activities helps cue children about what to expect, and provides extra support for participating meaningfully in classroom instruction.

Teachers can compile a **writing portfolio** to show progress over time, and to facilitate home communication and teacher/child dialogue about writing.

> ### Language Experience Approach
> Children dictate stories to the teacher (or aide), who writes them down. Children then copy the words that the teacher wrote. In this way, reading and writing become processes directly related to children's experiences. They read and write to express themselves and communicate their experiences.
>
> ### Dialogue Journals
> Dialogue journals develop writing skills and provide authentic communication between a child and teacher. This writing is informal, and may include pictures. It allows children to choose topics for writing. The teacher may suggest topics, but the choice is the child's. The child writes as in conversation with the teacher. The teacher responds to the content of the child's writing, also in a conversational manner. Writing errors are not explicitly corrected, but the teacher's writing serves as a model (Collier and Ovando, 1998).

Writing Products

While there are varieties of authentic writing assignments at each grade level that encourage children to write about their interests and experiences, there are specific genres with which children must become familiar in order to build an understanding of text structures that reflect district and state standards/curriculum frameworks. The following examples suggest ways to approach each genre in relation to English learners' needs in Grades 1 and 2. The blackline masters on pages 39–42 can be used to help English learners develop specific writing products.

A Story About Me

Have children use a **character web** to write about themselves and their experiences or what they can do and what they like to do. Provide a **word bank** of adjectives children at their grade level can use to describe themselves. Have children use a **story map** or **sequence chart** to plan. Guide them in deciding how to tell certain events. Have children **illustrate** the scenes in the chart first, and then give them **writing frames** for creating sentences that represent the scenes (In the beginning _____, etc.). (See page 39.)

How-to Report

Have children choose an activity that they or someone in their family knows how to do well. Ask children to use a **sequence map** to record the steps of the activity. Allow children to write the steps in their home language first, if that helps them organize their ideas. Provide **writing frames,** and have children insert words/phrases/sentences from their notes to create a How-to Report. (See page 40.)

Descriptive Paragraph

Have children choose a topic that interests them. Use an **idea web** to identify the topic, and brainstorm details about the topic. Encourage children to illustrate ideas they cannot yet express in English and help them add English words to the illustrations. Use **writing frames** to model the step-by-step writing of a descriptive paragraph. Have children write a descriptive paragraph at the same time the teacher models.

Persuasive Letter

Have children choose an argument. Often it helps children to think of an audience of someone they know, and so a personal note or letter provides an opportunity to write to persuade. Provide a **persuasive letter organizer.** Have children state the topic and then list reasons that support the point of view. Encourage children to illustrate (with simple drawings) ideas they cannot yet express in English. Then they can add English words to the drawings. Use **writing frames** to model the step-by-step writing of a persuasive letter. Have children write a persuasive letter after the teacher models. (See page 41.)

Compare and Contrast Essay

Have pairs of children compare their interests and experiences (languages they speak, home country or city, music, food, hobbies, goals for the future). Have partners **interview** each other, using a list of questions the class brainstorms. Then have them record what they have in common in the center of a **labeled Venn diagram**. Have them write what is different about each of them in the outer sections, separately labeled with their names. Provide **writing frames** to help children transfer information from the Venn diagram into a Compare and Contrast Essay format. (See page 42.)

Children learning to write will benefit from writing in their home language as well as the new language, English. They might write some compositions in both languages. Bilingual parents, staff members, and students can help children write in home languages.

Rubrics to Evaluate Writing

Teachers can use school, district, state, or national standards for English learners (which are aligned with English Language Arts standards) to create rubrics that adjust expectations for English learners based on their individual English proficiency levels.

The sample rubric on the following page focuses on one of the traits of good writing: rules (or conventions) of English. It describes what English learners at various levels (beginner, intermediate, and advanced) would be expected to write in the second half of Grade 1. Teachers can develop similar evaluation forms that reflect the needs of the school, the grade, and the children involved. Other examples of traits of good writing may include Focus/Ideas, Order, Writer's Voice, Word Choice, and Sentences. (See page 43 for a reproducible form.)

Traits of Good Writing: Rules (English Learners)

	Capitalization	Punctuation	Sentence Structure and Grammar	Spelling
Beginner (little experience in English)	Uses capitalization when writing one's own name.	Adds a period to the end of a sentence and a question mark to the end of a question.	Begins to use some standard word order, with mostly inconsistent grammatical forms (for example, subject/verb agreement).	Produces some independent writing that includes inconsistent spelling.
Intermediate (conversational but not academic English)	Uses capitalization to begin sentences and proper nouns.	Produces independent writing that may include some inconsistent use of periods and question marks.	Uses standard word order but may use inconsistent grammatical forms.	Produces independent writing that includes some misspellings.
Advanced (gaining skills in academic English)	Produces independent writing with consistent use of correct capitalization.	Produces independent writing with generally consistent use of correct punctuation.	Uses complete sentences and generally correct word order.	Produces independent writing with consistent use of correct spelling.

References

Collier, V. P., and C. J. Ovando (1998). *Bilingual and ESL Classrooms: Teaching in Multicultural Contexts*. Boston, MA: McGraw Hill.

Echevarria, J., M. Vogt, and D. Short (2004). *Making Content Comprehensible for English Learners: The SIOP Model*. Boston: Allyn & Bacon.

Fillmore, L. W., and C. E. Snow (2000). *What Teachers Need to Know about Language*. Washington, DC: ERIC Clearinghouse on Languages and Linguistics.

Vygotsky, L. S. (1978). *Mind in Society: The Development of Higher Psychological Processes*. Cambridge, MA: Harvard University Press.

Name _____

Story Map

Title _____

In the beginning	In the middle	At the <u>end</u>

Name _____

How-to Sequence Map

How to _____

Draw It

First _____

_____

Draw It

Next _____

_____

Draw It

Last _____

_____

Name _____

Persuasive Letter Organizer

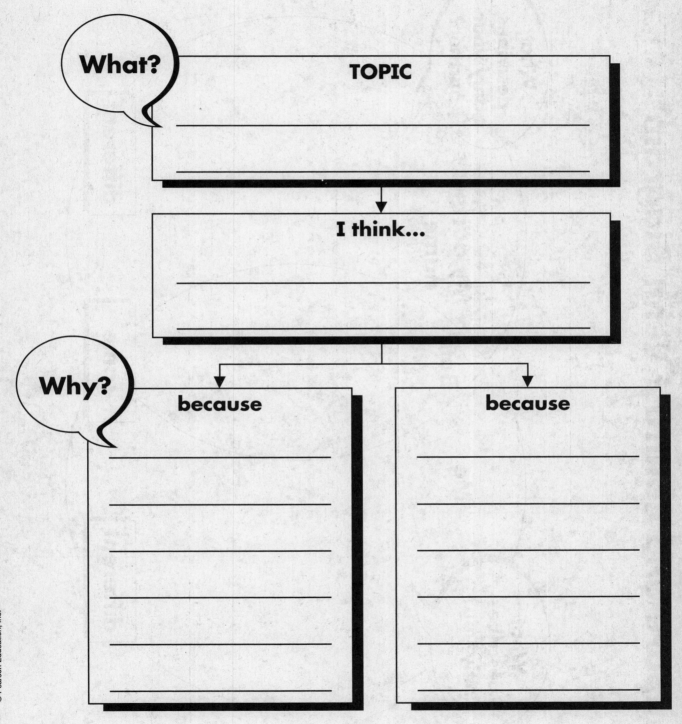

Name _____

Compare and Contrast Venn Diagram

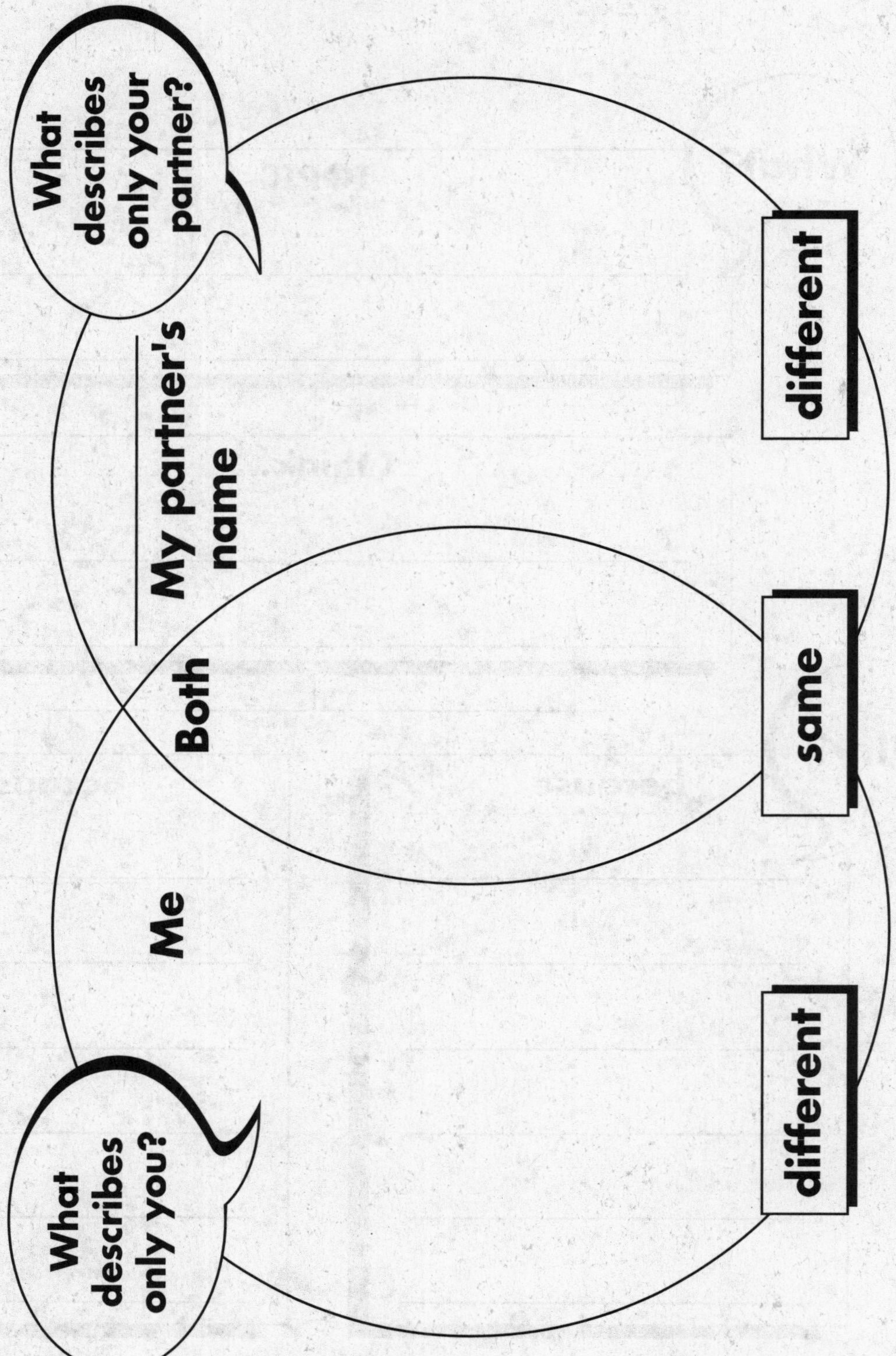

What describes only your partner?

My partner's name

Both

Me

What describes only you?

different

same

different

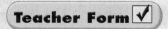

A Trait of Good Writing: _____
(English Learners)

_____ (trait)	_____	_____	_____
Beginner (little experience in English)	(Uses/Produces/Creates _____) _____ _____ _____ _____	(Uses/Produces/Creates _____) _____ _____ _____ _____	(Uses/Produces/Creates _____) _____ _____ _____ _____
Intermediate (conversational but not academic English)	(Uses/Produces/Creates _____) _____ _____ _____ _____	(Uses/Produces/Creates _____) _____ _____ _____ _____	(Uses/Produces/Creates _____) _____ _____ _____ _____
Advanced (gaining skills in academic English)	(Uses/Produces/Creates _____) _____ _____ _____ _____	(Uses/Produces/Creates _____) _____ _____ _____ _____	(Uses/Produces/Creates _____) _____ _____ _____ _____

Promoting Cultural Affirmation and Family Involvement

Research shows that a school curriculum that includes topics about children's cultures and experiences helps engage and motivate English learners. Teachers can use a variety of best practices to promote cultural affirmation and to draw upon parental involvement that supports children's learning.

- **Reflect Children's Cultures and Languages** Develop active learning and connections with the curriculum through the use of children's home cultures and, if possible, home languages. Plan reading, writing, speaking, and listening activities with texts that reflect children's personal interests, cultures, prior experiences, and background knowledge.

- **Link Curriculum to Home Resources** Create ways to use the home environment as an educational resource. Make connections between content area learning and the home through activities that depend on the expertise of family members. Use families' home languages and daily activities, such as cooking, cleaning, working, traveling, and playing, as a basis for learning.

- **Encourage Family Literacy** Plan family literacy activities that require children to interact with family members in the home language. Create a variety of activities such as discussion, telling or reading stories, listening to music or radio, and interviewing family members. Use these experiences as topics for discussion and sharing in the classroom.

- **Create School-Home Partnerships** Encourage parents to participate in their children's learning by planning school events that reflect the needs of parents or guardians of English learners. Plan activities and opportunities that show parents how they can use their home languages, their experiences, and their expertise both in the classroom and at home.

Family and Home as Educational Resources

- Get to know children's home lives and cultures by using everyday life and culture as topics for activities in class. Encourage storytelling and oral tradition by having children use their home languages to interview parents, grandparents, and immediate family members and then inviting children to share the stories with the class. Keep a portfolio of all the reading, writing, speaking, and listening activities that use children's home experiences, and compile them in binders that children can take home and show to their families.

- Use home activities for teaching concepts such as "following steps in a process" (for example, how to make something) and "giving directions." Ask children to find a special talent of a family member (for example, building or fixing something; singing, dancing, or playing a musical instrument; quilting, embroidering, or artwork; or cooking). Ask children to record (by writing notes or making pictures) the steps the family member performs. Help them turn their notes into instructions that other people can follow. Compile all the instructions in a class book to share with classmates and families.

- Create a class mural or quilt that represents the home cultures and languages of the children. Send home a panel for a mural or quilt, and ask the family to represent their culture and language through the use of visuals and/or writing. Encourage families to illustrate their special experiences and personalities (for example, by using a map of their home country, a family picture, words in the home language, artwork, or a souvenir or pictures from their home country and their travels). Hang the quilt or mural where parents can see it when they visit the school.

- Assign activities that include the use of families' home languages. These activities and assignments can utilize the home languages as well as the language of instruction, English. Have children ask family members for examples of children's rhymes or short songs in their home languages, and share these with the class. Help children explain in English, draw pictures for, or act out each home-language rhyme or song. As a class, brainstorm English rhymes or songs with similar themes or topics. Make a multilingual book of rhymes and songs to share with classmates and families.

Bridging the Curriculum and Home

- Plan family curricular events that combine social and curriculum-related themes when parents can come to see their children's presentations or projects. Plan hands-on math, science, and social studies related activities in which parents, siblings, and other family members can participate (such as astronomy night, math games, recipe exchange, and health fair). With the help of student journalists and photographers, create a monthly parent

newsletter, which includes pictures and descriptions of the kinds of activities children do in the different content areas.

- During parent conferences, home visits, or family events, provide information about daily class routines, and describe the classroom and school expectations for learners. List the strategies that will help children succeed in the classroom setting. Give examples of what the classroom expectations are, model how children should achieve them, and give children time to practice the strategies during appropriate times. Give parents and families information about ways they can support their children's learning at home (for example, *Ask your child to describe the activities he or she did in school; provide a quiet place where your child can read*). Send this kind of information to families in the home languages, and take time to discuss and review it at parent conferences and activities. Resources for home languages may include bilingual school staff, community members, and the families themselves.

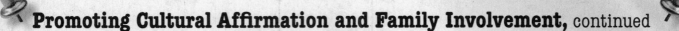
• Send a brief survey home to parents to find out more about their specific needs and concerns, and use this information to plan topics for family-based school events. Based on families' responses, invite guest speakers who speak the home languages of the families to give informational presentations about the topics of interest to families. Such activities tell families that the school is responsive to the needs of both children and their families as a whole, and that education is a partnership between home and school.

• Invite willing and able parents to be classroom helpers so they can learn how their children are taught specific subjects. Parent helpers then can reinforce at home the kinds of learning their children experience during school days. Parents can help the teacher and children during activities, can use their home languages to explain and assist, and can share relevant expertise with the class.

Links to Home Languages and Cultures

• Help children create dual-language books. Newcomers or beginners can write in their home languages; encourage children to gradually move into English, as they are able to do so. Such books can provide outreach to families with ranges of literacy backgrounds and can encourage children to make connections between their home languages and English.

• For math-related activities, collect and graph information about families' home countries or languages. Children can carry out simple interviews in the home language with family members and use target vocabulary and language for reporting information. Use a variety of graphs (bar, pie, and other kinds) to record information, and send class graphs home to share with families.

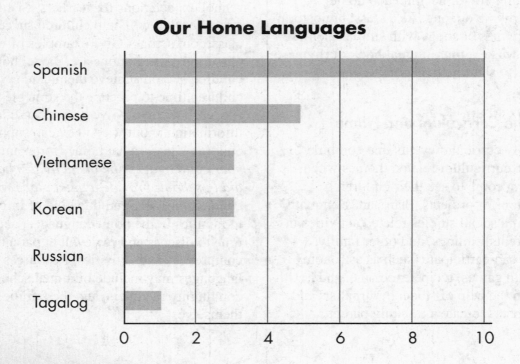

Our Home Languages

- Include family history, culture, and experiences as topics for projects. Have children interview family members and create a biography project. Invite children to include pictures, drawings, and stories that tell about families' home countries or cultures, ancestors, and customs. Celebrate by inviting families to school to share and read each others' biographies.

- Make "book bags" with audiobooks in home languages, and send them home to encourage family story activities. Encourage all family members to participate in home literacy activities. Provide a simple list of questions that families can discuss at home, and then ask children about their discussions.

References

August, D., and K. Hakuta. 1997. *Improving Schooling for Language Minority Children: A Research Agenda*. Washington, DC: National Academy Press.

Collier, V., and W. Thomas. 1992. A Synthesis of Studies Examining Long-Term Language Minority Child Data on Academic Achievement. *Bilingual Research Journal* 16(1-2): 187-212.

Cummins, J. 2000. *Language, Power, and Pedagogy*. Clevedon: Multilingual Matters.

Fillmore, L. W., and C. E. Snow. 2000. *What Teachers Need to Know about Language*. Washington, DC: ERIC Clearinghouse on Languages and Linguistics.

Freeman, Y. S., and D. E. Freeman. 2002. *Closing the Achievement Gap*. Portsmouth, NH: Heinemann.

Suárez-Orozco, C., and M. M. Suárez-Orozco. 2001. *Children of Immigration*. Cambridge, MA: Harvard University Press.

Helping the Helpers

Teacher assistants or aides, classroom volunteers, tutors, and classmates can provide important, ongoing support to students acquiring English. This support can be invaluable in helping students improve their proficiency.

How Can Teachers Recruit Helpers?

Invite parents, family members, school staff, and community members to be classroom helpers, in accordance with school or district policies. Contact community agencies that may coordinate and place volunteers in schools. Keep parents and the community updated through newsletters and announcements at school events about the specific opportunities and needs you have. College and university schools of education may be a good place to advertise volunteer opportunities, as students earning their teaching licensure are often interested in gaining experience in working with English learners.

You might use a school Web site to announce that you are looking for bilingual volunteers or for native English speakers who can spend time helping English learners improve their ability to read and write in English. You might identify students in your class who can show English learners certain classroom procedures, check that they understand activity instructions correctly, or listen to them read and help them with both pronunciation and comprehension. These peer helpers may include advanced English language learners who have acquired enough proficiency in English to offer help.

How Can Home Languages Be Used to Support English Learners?

Helpers who know the same home language as English learners can support instruction by clarifying key concepts and vocabulary and by reinforcing instructions and procedural information. Simultaneous or direct translation of what the teacher says is not recommended, since students should be listening to the teacher and pushing themselves to understand as much as they can. The helper, however, can listen with the student, check what the student understands, confirm what is correct, and add any details he or she may have missed. Volunteers also can use the home language to provide background knowledge that will help the student understand the overall meaning. Helpers also can use the home language as a way to connect classroom learning with students' prior experiences and cultural background.

Strategies for Classroom Instruction

The following chart lists a few strategies that volunteers can use when working with English learners. In the chart, L1 (Language 1) refers to the English learner's home language. When possible, find volunteers who know the home language of English learners. These volunteers can provide assistance to teachers and schools by communicating important instructional clarification to both the students and their families. Bilingual volunteers can facilitate the understanding of expectations and instructions, and they can provide clarification of subject matter concepts. Home language tutors also can provide information about the child's learning in the home language that will help the teacher more accurately assess the child's learning. Volunteers who primarily know the child's home language can provide support for the classroom teacher by developing children's home language literacy and learning skills, which will eventually transfer into English.

Adult Volunteer or Aide Helping in English	Adult Volunteer or Aide with L1 and English Fluency	Peer Helpers with L1, English, or Both	Adult Volunteer or Aide Helping Primarily in L1
____ Speak clearly and slowly. Learn to pronounce students' names correctly. ____ Use picture cards or other visuals to introduce and practice vocabulary. ____ Model pronunciation of new words and phrases, and have students repeat several times. ____ Use gestures, pictures, and objects when you give explanations to enhance understanding. ____ Give students extra time to understand your instructions or a question, and to give a response. ____ Read books with simple, repetitive, natural language that students can learn to read and use independently.	____ Support content-area learning by clarifying the meaning of concepts and vocabulary, in English and the home language. ____ Support hands-on activities by reinforcing teachers' instructions in English and in students' home language as needed. ____ Support communication with families by calling home to invite parents to school events, to remind them of important events such as picture day, and to provide details such as information about field trips. ____ Facilitate communication between English learners and the teacher when students need help expressing themselves in English.	____ Help students understand classroom rules and routines and the English terms and phrases associated with them. Show students how to follow teacher instructions. ____ Explain teacher's instructions or expectations in the home language. ____ Model reading, writing, listening, and speaking activities in English when working with partners or in small groups. ____ Convey questions or concerns that a newcomer may have to the teacher and communicate the teacher's answer to the student. ____ Be patient and encourage partner to keep trying. Smile!	____ Support students with reading, writing, speaking, and listening activities in the home language. ____ Record audio books for home-language book bags that can be used as home-language literacy activities. ____ Model storytelling in the home language, and encourage and listen to students' own storytelling in the home language. ____ Find ways to share the students' home culture and experiences with the teacher and classmates. Encourage projects such as a collage, a display, or another visual representation of the students' home culture.

English Language Learners and Assessment

Assessment Needs of Diverse Learners

Because English language learners make up a dynamic group of learners who enter school with a wide range of linguistic, cultural, and learning experiences, it is important for teachers to learn about the unique background of each individual learner. Overall, assessment can provide important information about children's learning that can be used to plan appropriate and meaningful instruction. However, the kinds of assessment, the purposes for which they are used, and how the results are evaluated can directly impact how meaningful the assessments are (Cummins, 1981).

High-stakes Testing vs. Authentic Assessment

While so-called "high-stakes" testing has become increasingly influential, high-profile tests can be difficult for English learners because they require proficiency in academic English, understanding of grade-level subject matter, and an understanding of cultural contexts. While high-stakes test results in the United States influence instructional decisions made in schools, these results often do not reflect **what** English learners know. Consequently, the instructional decisions based on test results often do not reflect the specific learning needs of English learners (Bielenberg and Fillmore, 2005).

It is important to find a variety of ways to assess English language learners that show what each child is able to do. Focusing on what children already know—and what they are learning but have not mastered—helps teachers identify the specific educational needs of children and enables educators to build their ongoing instruction upon all the resources, experiences, and abilities that English learners bring to school. Authentic assessment, or ongoing classroom-based (often informal) assessment of children by

teachers, allows children to show their strengths. Ongoing assessment also provides teachers with an accurate, dynamic picture of how to plan instruction and provide feedback in ways that meet the changing learning needs of each child (García, 1994). Following this approach, teachers can use accurate information about how to plan individualized instruction for English learners that will support their progress, through adaptations and modifications, until they are able to fully access and participate in the target curriculum in English and in assessments such as "high-stakes" tests.

Authentic Assessment Activities

Because English learners exhibit varying levels of English proficiency, it is important during assessment to allow them to express themselves in a variety of ways that do not depend solely on their understanding of English and their abilities to respond in English. The following is one example of this.

Story Retelling

Story retelling that allows children to support their verbal responses by drawing or illustrating details about the story (that is, to **show** the order of events in a story) can help the teacher assess what a child has understood, even if children do not yet have the vocabulary base or English language structures to describe the events in the story.

The following instructions describe how story retelling can be scaffolded, or specially structured, for English learners. It models the concept of sequencing events of a story by demonstrating sequential events with which children are already familiar, such as getting ready for school. This is one way to use informal assessment to find out whether individual children understand the concept of sequence, and whether they can use the sequence words appropriately to retell a series of events in order.

This story retelling activity also allows English learners to respond and express what they understand, according to their individual language proficiency level, by providing a variety of ways to express their understanding. English learners with beginning proficiency levels may use dramatization, illustrations, words, and possibly phrases to retell, while intermediate and advanced English learners may use a combination of the prior strategies along with sentences and possibly a short paragraph.

The Story Retelling Activity (page 56) that follows the instructions below can be used as a model form or adapted in order to meet the needs of children in various grades or with various levels of English proficiency.

Instructions: Story Retelling Activity (page 56)

Tell children that they will use the words *first, next, last* to retell a story that will be read or viewed in class, and let them know they will tell about the events of the story **in order**. This is one way to provide clear expectations that clue children in to what they will be asked to do, and it also provides background knowledge that can help children understand the story retelling process.

✓ Have each child repeat and practice the words *first, next,* and *last*. Provide an example of the meaning of these words by acting out what you do in the morning to get ready for school: "**First,** I wake up and eat breakfast. **Next,** I brush my teeth. **Last,** I walk out the door to go to school." Ask for volunteers to dramatize their own sequence of events (*e.g.,* a school day; shopping at the supermarket; getting ready for bed; etc.).

Write the words *first, next, last* on the board or on chart paper, and ask children to say the words as they are acting out their own sequence of events.

✓ After viewing, listening to, and/or reading a story, have children draw or illustrate what happened **first**, **next**, and **last** in the story that they will retell. For each scene illustrated, ask the child to describe what he or she drew. For those children who struggle with expressing the ideas in English, allow them to use the home language or encourage them to act out what they mean. Then write the word, phrase, or sentence that represents what they said in their home language or what they acted out.

✓ Record the responses: words (beginners), phrases (intermediate), or sentences (advanced). Finally, have each child copy what he or she dramatized, expressed in the home language, or dictated for each scene, on the lines below each scene. Ask children to repeat and practice the words, phrases, or sentences several times; then have them retell the story to a partner or to the whole group.

✓ For children with more advanced English language proficiency, add an extra column for an additional scene after "next" and label it "then." Ask them to include more detailed descriptions about the story. Encourage them to write several sentences for the scene in each column.

✓ As part of ongoing assessment of expressive reading and fluency, use audio equipment to record children's oral readings of the story retelling activity.

✓ To chart children's progress in story retelling, use the *Retelling Record teacher form* (page 57). To chart children's progress in the retelling of nonfiction selections, adapt page 56 for children to record ideas, and then use the Retelling Record on page 57.

Language Learning Profiles and Anecdotal Records

English language proficiency is acquired along a continuum. Individual learners often are at different places along this continuum, and they progress at different rates, based on a variety of factors such as proficiency in the home language, prior knowledge of English, similarities between the home language and English, motivation, learning styles, and prior literacy and learning experiences (August and Hakuta, 1997; Cummins, 1981). Because of the varying rates at which students acquire English, it is important for teachers to know and record where on the proficiency continuum each student is at the beginning of the school year (or when the student enters the school) and to keep ongoing observation records of student progress. This will not only help teachers recognize progress, but will also provide information about the specific areas in which English learners need extra support. Below is a general description of the different levels of English language proficiency.

Overview of English Language Proficiency Levels	
Beginning	Beginning English language learners have little vocabulary or literacy in English. This refers to their English proficiency, which is why it is helpful to learn as much as possible about children's literacy in their home languages.
Intermediate	Intermediate English learners have some conversational fluency in English but still are not proficient in the academic English of books and instruction.
Advanced	Advanced English learners have developed conversational fluency and some literacy/proficiency in academic English at their grade level, but they are not fully proficient and are still building their academic English.

Recording information about a student's proficiency in English and/or the home language can be done with the help of an initial **Language Proficiency/Literacy/Academic Profile** (see page 58). Checkmarks, notes, and dates can be used to fill in the chart. This form can be adapted to include content-specific or language-specific information. Through conferences with parents, and meetings with teachers, tutors, volunteers, and other specialists that work with English learners, teachers can continue to gather valuable information that will help inform instruction to provide individualized support for each child.

In addition to creating an initial **Language Proficiency/Literacy/Academic Profile** to gather background information and establish an understanding of the strengths an English learner brings to school, the use of **Anecdotal Records** (see pages 59 and 60) can provide ongoing assessment and information about children's learning that can show growth and inform the teacher about specific areas in which a child needs specific support and reinforcement.

When planning for instruction and assessing English learners, it is important to remember that these children are not only learning grade level subject area concepts, but they are also learning English language skills—reading, writing, listening, and speaking skills—at the same time. It is important that teachers include what children need to know and what they must be able to do with the language of instruction: vocabulary, language structures, procedural language such as asking questions, making predictions, describing, identifying, and so on. These language learning goals, or **language objectives,** help English learners develop language as well as content knowledge.

Teachers can use local and state standards developed for English learners and/or new national standards developed, for example, by Teachers of English to Speakers of Other Languages (TESOL), and the World-class Instructional Design and Assessment (WIDA) Consortium, a consortium of states that have created standards that describe what English language learners should be able to do at varying English language proficiency levels to achieve subject area learning. These standards can be used with the Anecdotal Record (page 60) under the "Skills" section to record reading, writing, speaking, and listening skills observed by the teacher.

Reading Fluency and Comprehension Assessment

Authentic assessment focuses on teachers making informed decisions based on authentic literacy tasks within the classroom context that reflect individual children's progress and learning (García, 1994). Finding ways to help English learners develop reading fluency means finding out if children really comprehend what they read, rather than just decode words. Reading comprehension depends on how well a child can extract meaning by making use of various clues in the text. Understanding and using clues in the text requires readers to be familiar with language structures, spelling, grammar, and text structures, and have background experience and knowledge about the topic of the reading passage.

Children's English language proficiency levels, the kinds of literacy and learning experiences children have had, and how familiar they are with the topic of the reading passage will affect how much they struggle with understanding what they read. Literature also can be challenging for English learners because of the use of figurative language, including metaphors, similes, and symbolism. Check children's reading comprehension and understanding of concepts such as *setting, characters, plot, beginning, middle,* and *end.* For example, ask a child to draw a picture of the setting of a story. Then ask the child to say or write words, a phrase or sentence, or several sentences about the drawing, depending on language proficiency level.

When assessing children's fluency and comprehension, it is helpful for teachers to learn how children's home literacy and languages affect their learning in English. English learners may draw on what they already know; for example, an English learner whose home language is Spanish may use Spanish spelling patterns and/or phonetics when reading or writing words in English. Recognizing the influence of the home language, and the child's reliance upon the literacy skills and strategies he or she knows in the home language, will help teachers not only assess more accurately, but know how to point out similarities and differences between English and the home language as a way to develop awareness about how different languages are related. This helps develop metalinguistic awareness, or thinking about how language works.

Teachers must ultimately use all they know about each child's English proficiency and literacy skills in order to:

- monitor progress
- organize children in groups for effective learning
- differentiate instruction.

Assessing English learners and learning about their cultural, linguistic, and learning experiences can help teachers become more precise in helping children and in planning instruction that is comprehensible and challenging.

Scaffolding High-stakes Testing

While "high-stakes" testing presents various challenges for English learners, there are various test-taking strategies that teachers can use to support children in preparing for eventual mastery of standardized testing. Showing children ways in which they can recognize test formats and decode the questions of a test will help them figure out what each question is asking them to do. Outcome based/norm referenced tests are different from ongoing authentic assessment because they evaluate, or make a judgment about, the performance of a child at a given time, while authentic assessment informs both teachers and children about day-to-day learning and provides feedback about how to proceed in order to meet the needs of individual learners.

English learners must be taught test-taking strategies and must build background about the language and procedures of test taking. Use the suggestions on the Test-taking Strategies Teaching Log (page 61) when preparing English learners, who may not be experienced with the specialized language and implications of standardized tests, to unlock the often hidden meaning embedded in test structure and language (Bielenberg and Fillmore, 2005).

Keep a log of ways to improve test-taking experiences for English learners. Teachers can refer to the log for future reference, for sharing with colleagues, and for self-assessing instruction for children. (See page 61.)

Here are instructions and examples for preteaching vocabulary and question types.

Preteach Vocabulary and Question Types

- Make a T chart to show examples of the question types children will find on tests. Explain what the structures mean and what they ask children to do.

- Make a short list of test vocabulary, phrases, and instructions children may find on tests—such as *choose, write, fill in the circle, less than, greater than,* and *"What event can really happen?"* Illustrate what these expressions ask children to do.

Example:

TEST DIRECTIONS	WHAT SHOULD I DO?
Choose the word that goes in the **blank**. **Mark** your answer. 1. Nancy rides her _____. O book O bike O store O gloves	• **Choose** = pick, decide on one • **Blank** = the line 1. Nancy rides her _____. • **Mark** = use pencil to fill in the circle

Example:

Instructions	What should I do?		
Find the **sum**.	Add numbers, + 10 + 1 = 11		
Compare the numbers using **>** , **<** , or **=**	<	less than	1 < 10
	>	greater than	9 > 2
	=	equals	3 = 3

Assessment Accommodations for English Learners

While English learners need time to acquire the academic language necessary to be able to practice and perform well on standardized tests in English, there are some accommodations that may support their attempts at extracting meaning from test language, questions, and passages. Accommodations for English learners may include the following:

- Provide English learners with extra time to complete the test.
- Allow the use of a bilingual dictionary or a picture dictionary to clarify words that may hinder comprehension.
- Read the question aloud in some cases.
- If possible, give the test in the classroom setting where children receive English learner services (if applicable) to reduce anxiety level.

References

August, D., and Hakuta, K. (1997). *Improving Schooling for Language Minority Children: A Research Agenda*. Washington, DC: National Academy Press.

Bielenberg, B., and L. W. Fillmore (2004–2005). The English They Need for the Test. *Educational Leadership, 62*(4), 45–49.

Cummins, J. (1981). The Role of Primary Language Development in Promoting Educational Success for Language Minority Students. In *Schooling and Language Minority Students: A Theoretical Framework*. Sacramento, CA: California Department of Education.

García, G. E. (1994). Assessing the Literacy Development of Second Language Students: A Focus on Authentic Assessment. In K. Spangenbergk-Urbschat and R. Pritchard (Ed.), *Kids Come in All Languages: Reading Instruction for ESL Students* (pp. 180–205). Newark, DE: International Reading Association.

Name _____

Story Retelling

Title _____

First

Next

Last

Retelling Record

Child's Name:

Behaviors Observed		Date:			Date:			Date:			Date:		
		Yes	Somewhat	No	Yes	Somewhat	No	Yes	Somewhat	No	Yes	Somewhat	No
Uses selection illustrations or photos to guide the retelling													
Adapts language heard in other retellings for his/her own purposes													
Provides additional information about the selection when questioned													
Fiction													
Identifies main characters and setting													
Describes significant events in the story													
Summarizes the ending of the story													
Nonfiction													
Uses text features such as headings, captions, diagrams, or labels to guide the retelling													
Identifies the main idea of the selection													
Identifies key details in the selection													

Language Proficiency/Literacy/ Academic Profile

Name _____ Grade _____

Home Language(s) _____

ABILITIES	Beginning	Intermediate	Advanced
L1 Listening			
L1 Speaking			
L1 Reading/Writing			
English Listening			
English Speaking			
English Reading/ Writing			
Academic/ Content Skills and Knowledge (English and L1)			

L1= Child's home language other than English

Anecdotal Record (Sample)

Child's Name and Date	Use of Oral English	Use of Written English	Skills	
Date: 5/3/06 **Child's Name:** *Mari* **English Language Proficiency Level:** ✓ Beginner — Intermediate — Advanced	*Asked Andre if she could borrow his scissors during centers work.*	*Copied friendly letter from overhead; used as a model to write the salutation of her own pen pal letter.*	**READING** *Follows list— instructions for writers workshop activity.*	**WRITING** *Records and labels objects that are blue.*
			LISTENING *Comprehends the high-frequency word "my."*	**SPEAKING** *Produces words and phrases to retell story.*

Anecdotal Record

Child's Name and Date	Use of Oral English	Use of Written English	Skills	
Date: _____ Child's Name: _____ _____ English Language Proficiency Level: __ Beginner __ Intermediate __ Advanced			**READING**	**WRITING**
			LISTENING	**SPEAKING**

Test-taking Strategies Teaching Log

How have I....?	Dates	Strategies and Activities
Pointed out the text structures and conceptual references used in tests in ways that children understand?		
Pointed out difficult language structures, grammar, and spelling?		
Pretaught basic vocabulary and content area vocabulary?		
Built background experience and knowledge about test taking and procedural language?		

Part 2
Grammar Instruction for English Language Learners

Contents

Introduction to the Grammar Transition Lessons

Young English language learners have experience mainly with their home languages, and the grammars of different languages vary widely. As these children encounter English, keep in mind that their home languages may differ in aspects such as the following:

- The languages may use different word order than English does.
- They may not use the same parts of speech as English does.
- Their tense structures may be simpler or more complex than English tense structure.
- Nouns and adjectives that are neutral in English may be masculine or feminine in a child's home language.

For teachers, it is vitally helpful to remember that grammar is much more than a set of rules for saying and writing sentences correctly. Grammar primarily consists of the ways that speakers and writers of a language communicate ideas, mainly in sentences. As children learn how English sentences work, along with the meanings of the words, they become able to successfully communicate their ideas. They will gradually learn the rules, read and write the punctuation, and eventually become proficient in the standard English usage that is regarded as correct English.

The core grammar and writing lessons in *Scott Foresman Reading Street* provide the systematic instruction that children need to write. The following Grammar Transition Lessons and Practice Pages will supplement the core instruction with customized lessons that meet the particular needs of English language learners.

Each group of grammar lessons covers a topic, such as Nouns, Verbs, or Sentences. Each lesson is supported by a reproducible Practice Page that provides strong context for the skill. Throughout the Grammar Transition Lessons, a **Transition to English** feature identifies challenges faced by English language learners, based on the grammar of their home languages, as well as language knowledge that can transfer to English. Each lesson also includes a **Grammar in Action** feature to reinforce the skill through active learning.

In addition to the Grammar Transition Lessons and Practice Pages, you can further support grammar instruction with routines such as the following:

- **Emphasize sentence meaning.** Encourage children to try to understand and convey ideas rather than focusing only on separate words. Build their knowledge by presenting many examples that show how English sentences communicate, including sentences that the children say or write.
- **Strengthen oral language skills.** Allow beginning English speakers to work with partners when completing grammar activities, talking about what English words and sentences mean. Encourage them to make up new phrases and sentences together.
- **Engage children as active learners.** Children who are acquiring English will make mistakes but need encouragement rather than constant correction. Let children take risks, communicate imperfectly, chant sentences, and have fun with English.
- **Relate to the home language.** Whenever possible, help children build on what they already know by making connections between a target grammar skill and the home language. Use available resources, such as bilingual staff members, language Web sites, and the children themselves, to gather information about the home language.

Nouns

Children's home languages also have words for people, places, animals, and things. To help them learn English nouns, bring items— apples, hats, dolls, stuffed toys, dishes, and so forth—for vocabulary building.

Grammar *in Action*

Noun Hunt Have partners look through picture books and say the nouns for people or things in the pictures.

Nouns

Introduce Point to objects in the room, and have children name them. Tell children: *We have names for the things around us. A noun is a word that names something or somebody.*

Teach Present the concept and provide examples:
- A noun names a person, a place, an animal, or a thing.

Person	Place	Animal	Thing
boy	school	bird	desk

Practice/Assess Copy and distribute page 68 or 69. Before children complete either page, read the directions aloud and name the items in the picture. (See answers on page 128.)

Proper Nouns
- Children whose home languages are non-alphabetic, such as Chinese, Korean, and Japanese, may need extra practice writing names with letters.
- In some Asian languages, family names appear first in persons' names. Point out that, in English, the family name follows the person's first name.

Grammar *in Action*

Special People and Places On chart paper, have children draw pictures and write or dictate the names of people and places that are special to them. Help them use capital letters.

Proper Nouns

Special Names

Introduce Have children practice writing their names. Point out that each child's name begins with a capital letter. Tell children: *Each of us has our own special name. A proper noun is the special name of a person, place, animal, or thing.* Then show children how to write names with capital letters.

Teach Present the concept and provide examples:
- A proper noun names a special person, place, animal, or thing.
- A proper noun begins with a capital letter.

Special Person	Special Place	Special Animal	Special Thing
Alex	Mexico	Fluffy	London Bridge

Practice/Assess Copy and distribute page 70 or 71. Before children complete either page, read the directions aloud and name the items in the picture. (See answers on page 128.)

Special Titles

Introduce Write the names of various school staff members on the board, including titles such as *Mr., Mrs.,* and *Dr.* Read the names aloud with children, and underline the titles as you say them.

Teach Present the concept and provide examples:
- A title can come before the name of a person.
- A title begins with a capital letter. Some titles end with a period.

Title	Example
Mr. *(mister)*	Mr. Lee
Mrs. *(missus)*	Mrs. Mills
Ms. *(miz)*	Ms. Lopez
Miss *(miss)*	Miss Witt
Dr. *(doctor)*	Dr. Po

Practice/Assess Copy and distribute page 72. Read the directions aloud before children complete the page. If appropriate, read the questions aloud. (See answers on page 128.) If appropriate, have children read their own answers aloud.

Days, Months, and Holidays

Introduce Ask children to name today's day and date. Write them on the board, and point out that the names of the day and month begin with capital letters.

Teach Present the concept and provide several examples:
- The names of the days of the week, months of the year, and holidays begin with capital letters.

Days of the Week	Months of the Year		Holidays (Examples)
Sunday	January	July	New Year's Day
Monday	February	August	Valentine's Day
Tuesday	March	September	Thanksgiving
Wednesday	April	October	
Thursday	May	November	
Friday	June	December	
Saturday			

Practice/Assess Copy and distribute page 73. Read the directions aloud. Go through the sample calendar with children before they complete the page. (See answers on page 128.)

© Pearson Education, Inc.

Transition to English

Titles
- Children may not realize that in English, the title *Doctor* is used for both men and women.
- For Spanish-speaking children, compare the titles *Mr., Mrs.,* and *Miss* to *Señor (Sr.), Señora (Sra.),* and *Señorita (Srta.).* Point out that in English, *Mr.* and *Mrs.* are almost always used before the person's name, not alone.

Grammar *in Action*

Introductions Have children practice introducing adult staff members to each other, using the correct titles.

Transition to English

Days and Months
In languages including Spanish, French, Polish, and Vietnamese, the names of days and months are not usually capitalized.

Grammar *in Action*

Capital Letters Sing this song to the tune of "Clementine": *Sunday, Monday, Tuesday, Wednesday, Thursday, Friday, Saturday. They start with capital letters, just like months and holidays.* Have children point to the names of the days on a calendar as they are mentioned.

© Pearson Education, Inc.

Transition to English

Plural Nouns

In some languages, including Chinese, Hmong, and Vietnamese, nouns do not have plural forms. Instead, the plural is indicated with an adjective.

Grammar *in Action*

Ten Fingers Pantomime this chant with children: *I have ten fingers. I have ten toes. / I have one mouth. I have one nose. / I have one chin. I have one head. / I have two eyes that close in bed.* List parts of the body under "one and more than one (with -s)."

Transition to English

Plural Noun Endings

Spanish-speaking children who have begun to read may be familiar with using -s and -es endings for plural nouns, as in the Spanish words for plants and flowers: *plantas* and *flores*.

Grammar *in Action*

Look Around the Classroom Sing to the tune of "Did You Ever See a Lassie?": *Please look around the classroom, the classroom, the classroom. Please look around the classroom, the classroom right now. Find boxes and lunches and glasses and brushes. Please look around the classroom, the classroom right now.* Have children find the items.

One and More Than One

Introduce Point to one book and say: *a book.* Point to two books and say: *books.* Repeat with *a girl* and *girls.* Have children name other singular and plural nouns as you point to them. Say: *Some nouns name one thing. They are called* singular nouns. *Some nouns name more than one thing. They are called* plural nouns.

Teach Present the concept and provide examples:
- Add -s to most nouns to form the plural, to tell about more than one.

One	More Than One
girl	girls
school	schools
dog	dogs

Practice/Assess Copy and distribute page 74. Help children name the singular and plural nouns in the picture. (See answers on page 128.)

Plural Nouns That Add -s and -es

Introduce Point to two chairs and say: *chairs.* Repeat with (lunch)boxes or other items represented by a plural noun with an -es ending. Tell children: *We usually add -s to form the plural. But if the noun ends in -ch, -sh, -s, -ss, or -x, we add -es.*

Teach Present the concept and provide examples:
- Most nouns add -s: *books, girls.*
- Some nouns add -es: *boxes, brushes, classes.*

Add -s	Add -es
girls	lunches
schools	dishes
dogs	buses
books	classes
teachers	boxes

Practice/Assess Copy and distribute page 75. Help children name the plural nouns in the picture. (See answers on page 128.)

Plural Nouns That Change Spelling

Introduce Say: The <u>children</u> brush their <u>teeth</u>. The <u>women</u> tap their <u>feet</u>. Tell children: *Most nouns add* -s *or* -es *to form the plural, but some change spelling to form the plural, like* children, teeth, women, *and* feet.

Teach Present the concept and provide examples:
- Most nouns add -s or -es: *books, girls, boxes, brushes.*
- Some nouns change spelling to form the plural.

child/children	foot/feet	life/lives	man/men
mouse/mice	tooth/teeth	wolf/wolves	woman/women

Practice/Assess Copy and distribute page 76. Help children name the plural nouns in the picture. (See answers on page 128.)

Transition to English

Irregular Plural Nouns
English learners may add -s to irregular nouns as they speak or write: *gooses, childrens, wolfs, clothings.* Provide practice with nouns that have different plural forms.

Grammar *in Action*

Share this poem; have children use plush toys or drawings of mice to act it out: *Past my feet ran two little mice. Or was it one mouse passing twice?*

Possessive Nouns

Introduce Give a book to each of three children. Stand by one child and lead the class in saying: *This is (child's name).* Then point to the book and say: *This is (child's name)'s book.* Repeat with the other children. Then have all the children show their books. Say: *These are the students' books.* Write the four possessive nouns on the board. Explain: *To show that a person, place, or thing has or owns something, add an apostrophe* (point to one) *and the letter* -s. *Just add an apostrophe* (point) *when the noun is plural and ends in* -s.

Teach Present the concept and provide examples:
- To form a possessive noun, add an apostrophe (') and -s when the noun is singular.
- Just add an apostrophe when the noun is plural and ends in -s.

S. Nouns	Possessive	Pl. Nouns	Possessive
friend	friend's name	children	children's books
girl	girl's book	cats	cats' bowls
school	school's library	puppies	puppies' toys

Practice/Assess Copy and distribute page 77. Help children read and understand the caption below each picture. (See answers on page 128.)

Transition to English

Possessive Nouns
In many languages, speakers show possession in phrases rather than noun endings. Show students how to change phrases such as *the tail of the bunny* to *the bunny's tail*, in order to show possession in English.

Grammar *in Action*

In Other Words Provide sentences such as these, and ask students to rephrase them using possessive nouns: *This book belongs to the girl. (This is the girl's book.) These chairs belong to the children. (These are the children's chairs.)*

© Pearson Education, Inc.

Picturing Nouns

Practice

- **Find** the people. **Circle** each person with a **blue** crayon.
- **Find** the animals. **Circle** each animal with a **red** crayon.
- **Find** the things. **Circle** each thing with a **green** crayon.

Assess

- **Talk** about the picture. **Name** some of the people, animals, and things you see in the picture.

Nouns
Practice

- **Look** at the picture.
- **Name** the people, places, animals, and things in the picture.

People	Places	Animals	Things
woman	zoo	zebra	tree

Assess

- **Look** around the room. What do you see?
- **Write** four nouns. **Name** things that you see.

Name _____

Picturing Proper Nouns
Practice

- **Draw** a picture of yourself. **Write** your name on the line.

My name is _____.

Assess

- **Say** the name of your friend: *My friend's name is....*

Name _____

Special Names
Practice

- **Look** at the picture. **Find** the people, animals, and places that have special names.
- **Write** the names. Begin with capital letters.

Names of People	Names of Animals	Names of Places
Tom		

Assess

- **Write** or **say** the names of two people you know.

_____

- **Write** or **say** the names of two special places you know.

_____

Name _____

Special Titles
Practice

- **Look** at the pictures. **Read** the questions.
- **Write** the name of each person.
- **Include** a title before each person's name.

Title	Use with:
Mr.	a man
Ms.	a woman
Mrs.	a married woman
Miss	an unmarried girl or woman
Dr.	a doctor (male or female)

Sara Mesa   Ed Green   Ann Cho   Sam Myers

1. Who is cooking? _____

2. Who is singing? _____

3. Who is helping a cat? _____

4. Who is teaching? _____

Assess

- **Write** or **say** the names of two adults you know. Include their titles.

_____

ELL and Transition Handbook

Name _____

Days, Months, and Holidays
Practice
- Use this class calendar to **answer** the questions.
- Remember to **begin** the names of days, months, and holidays with capital letters.

May						
Sunday	**Monday**	**Tuesday**	**Wednesday**	**Thursday**	**Friday**	**Saturday**
1	2	3 LIBRARY VISIT	4	5	6	7
8 Mother's Day	9	10 LIBRARY VISIT	11	12	13	14
15	16	17 LIBRARY VISIT	18	19 FIELD TRIP	20	21
22	23	24 LIBRARY VISIT	25	26	27	28
29	30 Memorial Day	31 LIBRARY VISIT				

1. What holiday is on Monday, May 30? _____

2. What holiday is on Sunday, May 8? _____

3. When is the field trip? _____

4. When does the class visit the library? _____

Assess

- In the United States, Mother's Day always falls on the same day of the week. **Write** or **say** the name of that day.

Name _____

One and More Than One

Practice

- **Look** at the picture.
- **Write** three singular nouns. **Write** four plural nouns.

Singular Nouns	Plural Nouns
tree	flowers

Assess

- **Look** around the room. What do you see?
- **Write** or **say** two singular nouns and three plural nouns.

Name _____

Plural Nouns That Add *-s* and *-es*
Practice
- **Look** at the picture.
- **Write** three plural nouns with *-s*. **Write** three plural nouns with *-es*.

Add *-s*	Add *-es*
swings	benches

Assess
Write or **say** the plural of *box*. Use this word in a sentence.

_____

Plural Nouns That Change Spelling

Practice

- **Look** at the picture.
- **Circle** three nouns that change spelling in the plural form.

Assess

Write or **say** the plural forms of these words: *man, woman,* and *child.*

Name _____

Possessive Nouns

Practice

- **Look** at the pictures. **Read** the words below.
- **Circle** the correct possessive nouns.

1. (Pals, Pal's) bowl

2. The (dogs', dog's) toys

3. The (cats, cat's) ball

4. The two (frogs', frog's) legs

Assess

- **Write** or **say** something that your classmate has.

Verbs

Transition to English

Action Verbs

English verb endings are simpler than verb endings in languages such as Spanish and Polish, which use different endings for person and number of subjects. Provide examples of English verbs with no added endings, used in sentences such as *We eat* and *They can run.*

Grammar *in Action*

What We Do Perform this cheer with children, acting out the verbs: *Action words tell what we do: swim, run, and talk to you! Sit, stand, and touch the sky! Jump, twist, and wave good-bye!* Brainstorm other actions for the cheer.

Transition to English

Verb Endings

Children who speak highly inflected languages such as Russian and Spanish may need practice adding -s to verbs in present tense with third-person singular subjects. Help children see the difference between -s on plural nouns and -s on verbs: *He bakes a pie; She runs.*

Grammar *in Action*

Charades Provide picture cards or word cards of verbs such as *eat, sleep, jump, run, wave.* Have children choose a card and pantomime the action for others to guess: *Gina waves; Gina runs.*

Action Verbs

Introduce Perform these actions as you narrate, and have children repeat your words and actions: *I clap. I walk. I sit. Which words tell what I do? (clap, walk, sit) A word that tells what we do is called a* verb.

Teach Present the concept and provide examples:
• An action verb tells what we do.

  I <u>play</u>. You <u>sing</u>. They <u>jump</u>. The dogs <u>bark</u>.

Practice/Assess Copy and distribute page 83 and/or 84. Help children understand each action verb. (See answers on pages 128 and 129.)

Verbs for Now

Verbs That Add -s

Introduce Gesture as you narrate: *She sits here. He sits here. She sees me. He sees me. The word* sits *is a verb. The word* sees *is a verb. A verb can tell what one person, animal, or thing does now. Many verbs that tell about now end in -s: sits; sees.*

Teach Present the concept and provide examples:
• Verbs in present tense tell what happens now.

  She <u>sees</u> me. He <u>sits</u>. The girl <u>runs</u>. The ball <u>rolls</u>.

Practice/Assess Copy and distribute page 85. Help children describe the picture. (See answers on page 129.)

Verbs That Add -s, -es

Introduce Say these sentences as you act them out (using the pronouns *his* and *He* if appropriate): *The teacher <u>touches</u> the board. The teacher <u>washes</u> her hands. She <u>passes</u> out papers.* Ask: *Which words tell what the teacher is doing? (touches, washes, passes)* Display the verbs and explain: *You know that we add -s to a verb to tell what a person, animal, or thing does. But sometimes we add -es to a verb. Some verbs are easier to say that way.* Challenge children to try adding only -s to *pass* or *wash*. Then have them add -es so they can hear the extra syllable: *passes, washes.*

Teach Present the concept and provide examples:
- Add -s to a verb to tell what a person, animal, or thing does.
- Add -es if the verb ends in *ch, sh, x,* or *ss.*

Add -*s*	jumps, plays, paints, runs, walks, eats
Add -*es*	teaches, washes, kisses, brushes, fixes

Practice/Assess Copy and distribute page 86. Remind children to add -es to some verbs. (See answers on page 129.)

Verbs That Do Not Add -s

Introduce Say these sentences, gesturing as you speak: *The children <u>play</u>. Two boys <u>jump</u> rope. Three girls <u>run</u>.* Ask: *Which words tell what they do? (play, jump, run)* Write the verbs on the board. Explain: *You know that we add -s to a verb to tell what <u>one</u> person, animal, or thing does. To tell what <u>two</u> or more people, animals, or things do, we do **not** add -s to the verb. Also, after the word I or the word you we do not add -s to the verb: I <u>walk</u> home. You <u>ride</u> the bus.*

Teach Present the concept and provide examples:
- Do **not** add -s to a verb that tells what two or more people, animals, or things do.
- Do **not** add -s to a verb that tells what I do or what you do.

  The men <u>plant</u> trees. The birds <u>sing</u>. You <u>play</u> a game.

Practice/Assess Copy and distribute page 87. Review the meanings of the verbs. (See answers on page 129.)

Transition to English

Present Tense
Help children recognize that -s and -es verb endings, although they are spelled differently, are similar. Provide examples in context rather than in word lists: *Ana rides a bike; Tom talks quietly; Mia brushes her hair; Dad fixes a lamp.*

Grammar *in Action*

In the Morning Teach children this song (to the tune of "On Top of Old Smokey"). Have them mime the actions: *Some days in the morning, Mom tickles my feet. She brushes my hair, and she kisses my cheek.* Think of other verses with *washes, fixes, teaches.*

Transition to English

Verbs with Plural Subjects
Guide children of various language backgrounds so they do not add -s to both the subjects and verbs, as in *The girls walks.* Help them practice saying and/or writing examples, such as *The girls walk, the boys smile,* and *we sing.*

Grammar *in Action*

-s or no -s? Write these words on cards: *The dogs, The girls, Max, My mom.* Write these verbs on another set: *sing, jump, run, play.* Have children draw a card from each set in order to create a sentence.

Verbs

Transition to English

Past Tense

In Chinese, Hmong, and Vietnamese, verbs do not change to show the tense. Instead, adverbs or expressions of time indicate when an action has taken place. Help children use past tense verbs in conversations.

Grammar *in Action*

Make It Past Display a list of verbs: *walk, play, jump, call, move, push, listen, watch.* Begin to tell a story: *Yesterday I walked to the park with my friend.* Have children add to the story, using the verbs from the list in the past tense.

Transition to English

Past Tense Ending

Assure children that the *-ed* ending for past tense verbs is always spelled *-ed,* regardless of how it is pronounced.

Grammar *in Action*

Verb Cube Make a verb cube by covering an empty box with paper. Write these verbs on the sides: *planted, waited, counted, melted, painted, visited.* Have children take turns tossing the cube. Invite them to say the verb, then use it in a sentence or act it out.

Verbs for the Past

-ed With the Sound of /t/ and /d/

Introduce Say these sentences, and display the verbs: *Yesterday, I walked to the park. I played with my dog. He barked at a cat. I pulled at his leash.* Explain: *I did these things yesterday, in the past. Many verbs that tell about the past end with* -ed. *Sometimes the* -ed *sounds like /t/, as in* walked *and* barked. *Sometimes the* -ed *sounds like /d/, as in* played *and* pulled.

Teach Present the concept and provide examples:
• Verbs in past tense tell what happened in the past.
• Many verbs in past tense end with *-ed.*

Sound of /t/	I asked her to play. We jumped rope. I helped her and she thanked me.
Sound of /d/	I opened the door and called your name. You cleaned your room.

Practice/Assess Copy and distribute page 88 after teaching the /id/ sound of *-ed,* below.

-ed With the Sound of /id/

Introduce Say, gesturing: *Yesterday, I visited my friend. We planted some flowers. I counted four flowers.* Display the verbs and explain: *I did these things in the past: visited, planted, counted. These verbs end with* -ed, *like the verbs we saw before. For these verbs, the* -ed *sounds like /id/. Listen: visited, planted, counted.*

Teach Present the concept and provide examples:
• Many verbs in past tense end with *-ed* that sounds like /id/.

Sound of /id/	I wanted my water to be cold. I needed some ice. I waited one hour. I lifted my glass. The ice had melted, so I added more ice.

Practice/Assess Copy and distribute page 88. Review the three sounds of *-ed.* (See answers on page 129.)

© Pearson Education, Inc.

Verbs for the Future

Introduce Say: *What will I do after school today? I will go home. I will eat an orange. I will play with my sister.* Explain: *Verbs can tell about action in the future. The future may be later today, next week, or even next year.* Write one of the statements and point out the word *will*. Say: *To talk about the future, put the word* will *before the verb.*

Teach Present the concept and provide examples:
- Verbs in future tense tell what will happen in the future.

I will visit Alicia.
We will see a movie.
Mom will drive me home.

Practice/Assess Copy and distribute page 89. Help children describe the picture. Review the meanings of the verbs. (See answers on page 129.)

Transition to English

Future Tense
Spanish, Haitian Creole, and Hmong speakers may use present tense in places where English calls for future tense. Help children practice verbs in statements such as *Tomorrow I will _____* and *After school, we will _____*.

Grammar *in Action*

Weekend Fun Brainstorm weekend activities, such as *play, visit, sleep, plant, read.* Ask: *What will you do this weekend?* Have children answer, starting with *I will* or *We will.* Invite children to pantomime the actions.

Am, Is, Are, Was, and Were

Introduce Make statements such as these: *I am your teacher. Lorena is a good student. Priya and Chong are friends.* Explain: *In these sentences, the verbs am, is, and are do not tell what someone does. They tell what someone is. Am, is, and are tell about now. Listen to these sentences: Yesterday was Tuesday. Two children were sick on Tuesday. Was and were tell about the past.*

Teach Present the concept and provide examples:
- Use *is* and *was* to tell about one person, place, animal, or thing.
- Use *are* and *were* to tell about more than one.
- Use *am* and *was* with *I.* Use *are* and *were* with *you.*

	am, is, are, was, were
Now	I am happy. You are happy. Celi is happy. The cat is happy. Celi and I are happy.
Past	Yesterday my lunch was good. My friends were hungry last night.

Practice/Assess Copy and distribute page 90. Help children describe the picture. (See answers on page 129.)

Transition to English

Forms of *to be*
- In Chinese, Hmong, and Haitian Creole, *to be* is not required in some sentences. If children say *I happy,* practice with sentences such as *I am happy* and *We are tired.*
- Tell Spanish speakers that English speakers say *We are hungry* rather than *We have hunger,* and *I am six years old* rather than *I have six years.*

Grammar *in Action*

Limbo Set up a game in which children try to walk under a stick without touching it. Have them chant: *Ed is smart. Ed is quick. Will Ed go under the big, long stick?* Play in pairs, using *are* in the chant.

© Pearson Education, Inc.

Verbs

Contractions
- Spanish-speaking children will know these contractions: *al = a + el; del = de + el.* Explain the apostrophe in English.
- In Spanish, Haitian Creole, and other languages, double negatives (comparable to *I did not do nothing*) are correct. Explain how *-n't* is used in English.

Grammar *in Action*

Say Again Display *don't, isn't, didn't,* and *aren't.* Have children rephrase these sentences using contractions: *Cats do not bark. That is not true. I did not know. My dogs are not big.*

More Contractions
Children may hear *I'm* and *it's* repeatedly but may not recognize them as contractions. Have children make these word cards: *I, am, I'm, it, is, it's.* Have them match the contraction to its words.

Grammar *in Action*

Together Sing together, and motion toward the subjects mentioned: *Now we're all together, together, together. Now we're all together, together right now. I'm here, and you're here, and she's here, and he's here. Now we're all together, together right now.*

Contractions with *Not*

Introduce Say and display these sentences: *I do not know. I don't know. These two sentences mean the same thing. The word* don't *is the words* do *and* not *put together. It is called a contraction. We can make a contraction by putting a verb together with the word* not. *An apostrophe takes the place of the o in* not.

Teach Present the concept and provide examples:
- A contraction is a short way to put two words together.
- An apostrophe takes the place of a letter or letters.

They <u>do not</u> see me.	They <u>don't</u> see me.
You <u>are not</u> walking.	You <u>aren't</u> walking.
I <u>did not</u> get a pen.	I <u>didn't</u> get a pen.
That <u>is not</u> my dog.	That <u>isn't</u> my dog.

Practice/Assess Copy and distribute page 91. Help children describe the picture. (See answers on page 129.)

More Contractions

Introduce Say these sentences: *I am your teacher. I'm your teacher. I said the same thing twice. In the second sentence, I made a contraction from* I am. *We can make a contraction with a pronoun,* such as I, you, he, she, or they. *Put it with a verb such as* am, will, are, *or* is.

Teach Present the concept and provide examples:
- Make a contraction with a pronoun plus *am, will, are,* or *is.*

If <u>you are</u> going, <u>I am</u> going too.	If <u>you're</u> going, <u>I'm</u> going too.
<u>She is</u> my sister.	<u>She's</u> my sister.
<u>You are</u> my friend.	<u>You're</u> my friend.
<u>I will</u> go now.	<u>I'll</u> go now.

Practice/Assess Copy and distribute page 92. Read the items with both answer choices. (See answers on page 129.)

Name _____

Picturing Verbs
Practice

- **Draw** a picture of yourself playing.
- **Draw** a picture of yourself sitting.

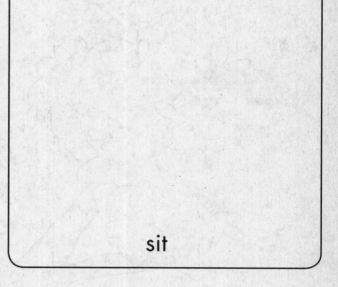

play

sit

Assess

- **Think** of something else you can do. **Draw** a picture of yourself doing it.

Name _____

Action Verbs
Practice

- **Look** at the picture. **Read** the sentences.
- **Circle** the action verb in each sentence.

1. I sit in my yard.

2. The birds sing.

3. I look at the birds.

Assess

- **Write** or **say** a sentence about what you do. Use one of these action verbs: *eat, read, play, run*.

Name _____

Verbs That Add -s
Practice
- **Look** at the picture. **Read** the sentences.
- **Circle** the correct verb to complete each sentence.

1. Ray (kick, kicks) the ball.

2. Lucy (runs, run) fast.

3. Max (stop, stops) the ball.

Assess
- **Look** at the picture. **Write** or **say** a sentence about the mom. Use *claps* or *sits*.

Name _____

Verbs That Add *-s, -es*
Practice
- **Look** at the picture. **Read** the sentences.
- **Write** the correct verb to complete each sentence.

doll

1. Mom _____ Lili's doll.   (fix, fixes)

2. Lili _____ Mom.   (huges, hugs)

3. Lili _____ Mom.   (kiss, kisses)

Assess
- **Look** at the picture. **Say** another sentence about the doll. Use the verb *washes*.

Verbs That Do Not Add -s
Practice
- **Look** at the picture. **Read** the sentences.
- **Circle** the correct verb to complete each sentence.

1. Tim and I (ride, rides) our bikes.

2. Mom and Dad (run, runs) on the path.

3. Tim (sing, sings) a silly song.

4. I (smile, smiles) at the song.

Assess

Write or **say** a sentence about Mom and Dad. Use the verb *sing*.

_____

Verbs for the Past
Practice

- **Look** at the picture. **Read** the sentences.
- **Circle** the correct verb to complete each sentence.

bowl

1. Yesterday, I (visit, visited) my grandmother.

2. We (bakes, baked) cookies.

3. I (cleaned, cleans) the bowl with my finger.

Assess

Have you ever helped in the kitchen? **Write** or **say** a sentence about it. Use *cooked* or *baked*.

Verbs for the Future
Practice

- **Look** at the picture. **Read** the sentences. **Read** the verbs in the box.
- **Write** the correct verb that tells about the future.

Mama duck _____ her babies to swim.

Soon, the baby ducks _____ big and strong.

They _____ in the pond with no help.

will swim	will teach	will grow

Assess

- What do you think will happen when the baby ducks are grown? **Write** or **say** a sentence about it.

_____

Name _____

Am, Is, Are, Was, and Were
Practice
- **Look** at the picture. **Read** the sentences.
- **Circle** the correct verb in each sentence.

1. Yesterday, I (are, was) sick.

2. Today I (am, are) still sick.

3. Last week, my sisters (was, were) both sick.

4. Mom (is, are) very nice to me.

5. She and I (are, is) talking.

Assess
- **Write** or **say** a sentence about the sick girl. Use the verb *is*.

© Pearson Education, Inc.

Name _____

Contractions with *Not*
Practice

- **Look** at the picture. **Read** the sentences.
- **Write** the contraction for the underlined words.

umbrella

1. Oh, no! I <u>did not</u> bring my umbrella. _____

2. It <u>was not</u> raining this morning. _____

3. I <u>do not</u> want to get wet! _____

Assess

- **Write** or **say** a sentence about getting wet. Use one of these contractions: *don't*, *didn't*, or *isn't*.

_____

© Pearson Education, Inc.

More Contractions
Practice

- **Look** at the picture. **Read** the sentences.
- **Circle** the correct contraction to complete each sentence.

1. (I'm, I'll) going out to play.

2. (She's, I'll) play with you!

3. Thanks! (You're, You'll) the best, Dad!

Assess

- **Write** or **say** a sentence about the boy. Use the contraction *he's*.

Meaningful Word Groups

Phrases

Introduce Say and write these words on the board: *dog, little,* and *the*. Ask: *What do these words mean? Let's look at them one at a time. The first word names a kind of animal. The second word tells a size. The word the by itself doesn't tell me anything. These words are like pieces of a puzzle. They don't mean very much when they are put together this way. Look what happens when I arrange the words differently:* the little dog. *These words really mean something when they are put together this way. They help me think of a little dog.*

Teach Present the concept and provide examples:
- Meaningful word groups make sense when we say or read them together.

Meaningful:	a red cat	sat on a mat
Not meaningful:	cat my a	red a sat

Practice/Assess Copy and distribute page 99 after the second lesson on Meaningful Word Groups (below).

Sentences

Introduce Write these words on large cards: *dog, away, ran,* and *the*. Say them and post them on the board: Ask: *Do these words tell us anything? Can we arrange these words so that they do tell us something?* The dog ran away. *Now these words tell us something. They tell us that the dog ran away. We put these words together so they would tell us something. We made a sentence.* Write the sentence on the board. *When you write a sentence, it starts with a capital letter. It ends with a dot called a period.*

Teach Present the concept and provide examples:
- A meaningful word group that tells something is called a *sentence*.

Meaningful:	A fat cat can run.
Not meaningful:	cat run can A fat

Practice/Assess Copy and distribute page 99. Read the words together. Remind children what a sentence looks like. (See answers on page 129.)

Transition to English

Putting Words Together
Meaningful word groups in English may not always be self-evident to children whose home languages may use different patterns of word order. Restate children's sentences to help familiarize them with correct word order in English.

Grammar *in Action*

Puzzle Pieces Write phrases such as these on cardstock: *The yellow cat / My red car / runs fast.* Cut each phrase apart into large puzzle pieces. Mix them up. Read each piece randomly. Help children put the pieces together so they form meaningful word groups.

Transition to English

Meaningful Sentences
Help children understand that sentences in English should make sense—and they will understand English sentences more and more as they learn more English words.

Grammar *in Action*

Word Cards Write these words on individual cards: *on the sat A cat bed*. Have children draw a card and hold the card up. Read each card, and make sure children know the meaning of each word. Help children arrange themselves to make the sentence *A cat sat on the bed*.

Naming Parts of Sentences (Subjects)

Introduce Say this sentence: <u>The girl</u> walks to school. Ask: *Who is this sentence about? (the girl)* Explain that "The girl" is the naming part of the sentence. It tells whom or what the sentence is about. The naming part is called the *subject* of the sentence. It can tell who or what does something.

Teach Present the concept and provide examples:
- The naming part, or subject, tells who or what the sentence is about.

    <u>Mom</u> made cookies. <u>Lisa</u> ate a cookie. <u>The cookie</u> broke.

Practice/Assess Copy and distribute page 100 and/or 101. Before children complete either page, read the directions aloud and help them name the items in the picture. (See answers on page 129.)

Action Parts of Sentences (Predicates)

Introduce Say this sentence again: *The girl walks to school.* Ask: *What does the girl do? (walks to school)* Explain that this is the action part of the sentence. It tells what a person or thing does. The action part is called the *predicate* of the sentence.

Teach Present the concept and provide examples:
- The action part, or predicate, of a sentence tells what the subject does.

    We <u>walk home</u>. Mom <u>drives the car</u>. We <u>go to the store</u>.

Practice/Assess Copy and distribute page 102 and/or 103. Before children complete either page, read the sentences aloud and help them describe each picture. (See answers on page 130.)

Word Order

Introduce Display these sentences and read them aloud, gesturing: *The bird flies. Flies the bird.* Ask: *What is the naming part of the first sentence?* (The bird) *The second sentence does not sound right. The words are not in the right order to make a sentence. In an English sentence, the naming part usually comes first. The action part usually comes after the naming part.*

Teach Present the concept and provide examples:
- Sentences need to have words in the right order.
- In a statement, the naming part usually comes first. The action part usually comes next.

In the right order:	The dog barks.
Not in the right order:	Barks the dog.

Practice/Assess Copy and distribute page 104. Help children describe the picture. (See answers on page 130.)

Transition to English

Word Order

Help students see that word order strongly affects meaning in English. *The puppy barked at Kay* has a different meaning from *Kay barked at the puppy.* Have children practice changing the word order in sentences to express different meanings.

Grammar *in Action*

Correct Order Help partners make cards with parts of sentences: *My friend / rides a bike. Rides a bike / my friend. Plays / the dog. The dog / plays. The bird / sings. Sings / the bird.* Have partners say the parts and build sentences in correct word order.

Complete Sentences

Introduce Display and read these groups of words: *Tom went to the library. To the library.* Say: *The first group of words is a sentence. What is the naming part?* (Tom) *What is the action part?* (went to the library) *The second group of words, "to the library," is not a complete sentence. There is no naming part or action part. A complete sentence needs a naming part and an action part.*

Teach Present the concept and provide examples:
- A complete sentence needs a naming part and an action part.

Complete	Rai eats lunch.
Incomplete	Her lunch in a bag.

Practice/Assess Copy and distribute page 105. As an extension, have children choose a fragment from the Practice and create a sentence from it. (See answers on page 130.)

Transition to English

Complete Sentences

In Spanish and Chinese, speakers do not need to include some pronouns as sentence subjects because the context may make the pronoun unnecessary. Have students practice including such pronouns in English.

Grammar *in Action*

Complete or Incomplete? Read these groups of words. Have children raise their hands each time they hear a complete sentence. *My brother. We walk to school. We ride the bus. In the car. After school.* Invite children to say sentences.

Transition to English

Statements

Children who read in Spanish may recognize that a sentence begins with a capital letter and ends with a period. The Spanish word for "capital letter" is *mayúscula*, and the period is called *punto* (which can mean "point," "dot," or "period").

Grammar *in Action*

Make a Statement Make sets of cards such as these: The cat / sees / the bird. / The bird / sees / the cat. Mix the cards, and have children form statements. Remind them to put the capital letter at the beginning and the period at the end.

Types of Sentences

Telling Sentences

Introduce Display and read these sentences: *We jump rope. My brother plays with cars.* Say: *Let's look at these sentences. Each one starts with a capital letter and ends with a period. Each one tells something, so it is a telling sentence. A telling sentence is called a* statement. *It states, or tells, something.*

Teach Present the concept and provide examples:
- A sentence that tells something is called a *statement*.
- It begins with a capital letter and ends with a period.

Statements

That cat is black.
My mom likes cats.
We have two cats.

Practice/Assess Copy and distribute page 106. Remind children that a statement begins with a capital letter and ends with a period. (See answers on page 130.)

Transition to English

Questions

- Help children understand that questions in English often begin with words such as *who, what, when, where, how, do,* and *did.*
- Speakers of Asian languages often form questions by adding words to statements, comparable to *The water is cold, no?* Provide extra practice with English questions.

Grammar *in Action*

Ask Me Have children ask each other questions about what they did yesterday. For example, *What did you eat for lunch? Who played games with you?*

Questions

Introduce Say: *Listen to these sentences: What is your name? Where do you live? How old are you? Do you have any cats?* Ask: *How are these sentences different from statements? They each ask something.* Write two of the sentences on the board. Ask: *How else are they different? Each one ends with a question mark. A sentence that asks something is called a* question.

Teach Present the concept and provide examples:
- A sentence that asks something is called a *question*.
- It starts with a capital letter and ends with a question mark.

Questions

How are you?
What is your teacher's name?
Where is your school?

Practice/Assess Copy and distribute page 107. Help children describe the picture. (See answers on page 130.)

Exclamations

Introduce Write and say in an excited voice: *I am very happy!* Have children repeat, and then ask: *What feeling does that sentence tell about? (excitement; happiness) Whenever you say something with strong feeling, you are saying an exclamation. A written exclamation begins with a capital letter and ends with an exclamation mark.*

Teach Present the concept and provide examples:
- An exclamation is a sentence that shows strong feeling.
- It begins with a capital letter and ends with an exclamation mark.

Exclamations
This is fun! This swing goes high! I can touch the sky!

Practice/Assess Copy and distribute page 108. Practice intonation of exclamations. (See answers on page 130.)

Transition to English

Exclamations
The exclamation mark at the end of an exclamation is the same in English and Spanish. Tell Spanish-speaking students that, in English, there is no exclamation mark at the beginning of the sentence.

Grammar *in Action*

With Emotion Say these sentences and have children repeat them as exclamations: *That dog is big. He is barking. I can't hear you.*

Commands

Introduce Give children various commands such as these: *Please stand up. Walk to the front of the class. Say hello. Sit down.* Ask: *How are these sentences the same? In each one, I am telling you to do something. A sentence that tells someone to do something is called a command. It begins with a capital letter and ends with a period.*

Teach Present the concept and provide examples:
- A command is a sentence that tells someone to do something.
- It begins with a capital letter and ends with a period.

Commands
Come to my house. Play with me. Draw me a picture.

Practice/Assess Copy and distribute page 109. Read the sentences aloud. (See answers on page 130.)

Transition to English

Commands
Help children recognize that, in English, a command usually does not state the person ("you") who is commanded to do something. English commands also may not state that the action should be done now. "Please take this to the office" means "(You) please take this to the office (now)."

Grammar *in Action*

1, 2: Tie Your Shoe Share this poem. Have children mime the actions mentioned in the commands: *1, 2: Tie your shoe. 3, 4: Touch the floor. 5, 6: Pick up sticks. 7, 8: Close the gate. 9, 10: Twist and bend.* Brainstorm other rhyming commands.

© Pearson Education, Inc.

Transition to English

Compound Sentences
Children may have difficulty seeing the clauses in a compound sentence. Point out the conjunction (and; but) in the examples. Give additional practice finding the subject and verb within independent clauses.

Grammar *in Action*

Commas in Compounds Write these sentence pairs on sentence strips: *Juanita likes cats. She doesn't like dogs. / Ana loves animals. She has many pets.* On cards, write *and, but*, and two commas. Distribute cards and sentence strips, and have children join the sentences with a comma plus *and* or *but*.

Transition to English

Commas in Dates
Children may be familiar with dates in which the day number comes first, as in *4 July 1776.* Show how the comma helps separate the day number from the year number in dates as written in the United States.

Grammar *in Action*

All About Me Have children write sentences about themselves using these models: *I was born on February 7, 1997. I was born in Houston, Texas.*

Compound Sentences and Commas

Introduce Display and read these sentences: *I went to Mimi's house. We ate lunch.* Explain: *These two sentences have ideas that go together. We can join them to make a longer sentence:* I went to Mimi's house, and we ate lunch. *Here's what to do (demonstrate as you talk): Take out the period in the first sentence; put in a comma instead. Add* and. *Add the second sentence, starting with a lowercase letter. To join sentences that have opposite ideas, use* but: I went to the library, but it was closed.

Teach Present the concept and provide examples:
• A compound sentence has two sentences joined by a comma and the word *and* or *but.*

Simple Sentences	I am 8 years old. I am in the second grade. Joe likes bikes. He does not have one yet.
Compound Sentences	I am 8 years old, and I am in the second grade. Joe likes bikes, but he does not have one yet.

Practice/Assess Copy and distribute page 110. In the first compound sentence, help children see the two simple sentences. (See answers on page 130.)

More About Commas

Introduce Display these examples: *July 4, 1776. Thursday, July 4. Chicago, IL 60626. I like blue, red, and yellow.* Explain: *Commas tell us where to pause, or slow down. We use commas in many ways. We use commas in dates. We use commas in addresses. We use commas to separate three or more things in a list.*

Teach Present the concept and provide examples:
• Use commas in dates: *February 14, 1963*
• Use commas in addresses: *Salinas, CA 93908*
• Use commas to separate three or more things: *Ben, Alma, and Cindy went home.*

Practice/Assess Copy and distribute page 111. Read the sentences, and pause where the commas belong. (See answers on page 131.)

Meaningful Word Groups
Practice

- **Read** each group of words.
- **Draw** what each group means.

a big cat	The big cat has a hat.

Assess

Which of the word groups is a sentence? **Point** to it, and **read** it aloud.

Name _____

Picturing Sentences: Naming Parts
Practice

- **Read** the sentence.
- Who or what is the sentence about? **Color** that animal in the picture.

The dog likes to run.

Assess

- **Say** a new sentence using the same naming part.

© Pearson Education, Inc.

Name _____

Naming Parts of Sentences (Subjects)
Practice
- **Look** at the picture. **Read** the sentences.
- **Circle** the naming part of each sentence. It is the subject.

1. Mom opens a can.

2. Ted gets the pan.

3. The pan is on the top shelf.

Assess
- **Write** or **say** a new sentence. Use the naming part of one of the sentences above.

Picturing Sentences: Action Parts
Practice

- **Read** the sentence.
- What is the action part? **Circle** the picture that shows the action.

Dad sat in the sun.

Assess

- **Say** a new sentence about yourself. Use the same action part.

Action Parts of Sentences (Predicates)

Practice

- **Look** at the picture. **Read** the sentences.
- **Circle** the action part of each sentence. It is the predicate.

1. I play with my cat.

2. A dog barks at him.

3. My cat runs away.

Assess

- **Write** or **say** a new sentence. Tell what happens next.

Word Order
Practice

- **Look** at the picture. **Read** the sentences.
- **Circle** the sentences with the words in the right order.

1. I drew a picture.
  Drew a picture I.

2. This is my house.
  My house this is.

3. Is green and white my house.
  My house is green and white.

Assess

- **Look** at the picture again. **Say** another sentence about it.

Complete Sentences
Practice

- **Look** at the picture. **Read** the groups of words.
- **Circle** each group of words that is a complete sentence.

1. How the woman.   The woman sells oranges.

2. She cuts the oranges.   Lemons and oranges at the market.

3. Oranges and lemons.   You can buy honey too.

Assess

- **Choose** one of the incomplete sentences. **Add** more words to make a complete sentence.

Name _____

Telling Sentences
Practice

- **Look** at the picture. **Read** the sentences.
- **Write** each telling sentence correctly.

1. this is Lobo's party

_____

2. we gave Lobo a new toy

_____

3. we had a cake

_____

4. Lobo had fun

_____

Assess

- **Write** or **say** another statement about Lobo's party.

_____

Questions
Practice

- **Look** at the picture. **Read** the sentences.
- **Circle** each question.

1. I do not see you.   Where are you?

2. Are you here?   I will find you.

3. I see you by the tree.   Can you run fast now?

Assess

- Pretend you are looking for the boy. What would you ask?
  Write or **say** the question.

Name _____

Exclamations
Practice
- **Look** at the picture.
- **Write** the exclamation that each person says.

Push me too!
I am going high!
My arms are tired!

Assess
- What would you say if you were going fast?

Commands

Practice

• **Look** at the pictures.
• **Circle** the sentences that are commands.

1. This is how to make a sandwich.

2. Put peanut butter on a slice of bread.

3. Put jelly on the other slice.

4. It's easy!

Assess

• **Write** or **tell** how to make a peanut butter and jelly sandwich. Use commands. Use these words: *get, put, cut, eat.*

_____

_____

Compound Sentences and Commas
Practice

- **Look** at the pictures. **Read** each sentence.
- **Add** a comma where it is needed in each sentence.

1. Dad made a birdhouse and I will put it in the tree.

2. I got the hammer and nails but only Dad used them.

3. Dad made the birdhouse and now we can paint it.

4. We look all over but we do not see the paintbrush!

Assess

- **Read** the compound sentences aloud. Pause at each comma.

Name _____

More About Commas

Practice

- **Look** at the picture. **Read** the sentences.
- **Add** commas to the sentences.

We took a trip on May 14 2005. We went to Santa Barbara California. We saw Rosa Gus Maria and Eva. We came home on Sunday May 22.

Assess

- **Write** or **say** a sentence about a place you visited. Name three things you saw there.

Adjectives and Adverbs

Transition to English

Color Names
- Help children learn the English words for colors through many encounters.
- Speakers of Polish and other languages may express choices among objects using adjectives without nouns: "I want the blue." Help children add the noun.

Grammar *in Action*

Clothes Sing to the tune of "Frère Jacques," having children call out different colored clothing each time: *Who is wearing a red sweater? Please stand up. Please stand up. Show us your red sweater. Show us your red sweater. Thank you very much. Thank you very much.*

Transition to English

Shapes
Help children understand that the word *square* can be used both as an adjective and as a shape name (noun). The word *round* is an adjective, but the shape name is *circle*.

Grammar *in Action*

My Monster Have partners take turns describing a monster for the other to draw: *Draw two round heads. Draw a square body. Draw three oval eyes.* Afterward, have children show their monsters and describe them to the class.

Adjectives

Adjectives for Colors

Introduce Display a box of crayons. Pull out a crayon as you point out items in that color: *This is a red crayon. What else in this room is red? Ah, here is a red book.* Repeat with other colors. Explain: *The words* red, yellow, blue, green, orange, brown, purple, *and* black *tell more about things. They are adjectives. Adjectives tell more about a person, place, or thing. Some adjectives are the names of colors.*

Teach Present the concept and provide examples:
- Some adjectives name colors.

yellow house, **red** apple, **blue** car, **green** grass, **orange** crayon, **brown** shoe, **purple** ball, **black** cat

Practice/Assess Copy and distribute page 116 and/or 117 after teaching *Adjectives for Shapes.*

Adjectives for Shapes

Introduce Point out items in the room as you draw their shapes in the air with your finger: *Here is a round rug (or clock). What else is round? Here is a square block. What else is square?* Explain: *The words* round *and* square *are adjectives. Some adjectives name shapes.*

Teach Present the concept and provide examples:
- Some adjectives name shapes.

round circle, **round** dot; **square** window, **square** paper; **oval** egg

Practice/Assess Copy and distribute page 116 and/or 117. Before children complete either page, review color words and shape words. (See answers on page 131.)

© Pearson Education, Inc.

Adjectives for Size

Introduce Display pictures of animals of various sizes: *Here is a small mouse. Here is a big whale. A giraffe has a long neck. A turtle has short legs.* Explain: *Some adjectives describe size.* Big, small, long, *and* short *are just a few of the adjectives that describe the size of a person, place, animal, or thing.*

Teach Present the concept and provide examples:
• Some adjectives describe size.

big man, **small** dog, **long** line, **short** tree

Practice/Assess Copy and distribute page 118. Discuss the characteristics of each animal. (See answers on page 131.)

Transition to English

Adjectives for Size
In Spanish and Vietnamese, adjectives may follow nouns, as in the name *Río Grande* ("big river"). Help children write adjectives before nouns in English.

Grammar *in Action*

What Am I? Review words for animal body parts, such as *tail, head, ears, eyes, legs.* Have children give animal clues for a partner to guess: *I am a small animal. I have long ears. I can hop.* (rabbit)

Adjectives for What Kind

Introduce Point out items in the room as you describe them: *This is an old table. What kind of table is this?* (old) *This is a new book. What kind of book is this?* (new) Continue with other items around the room. Explain: *The words* old *and* new *are just a few adjectives that tell what kind.*

Teach Present the concept and provide examples:
• Some adjectives tell what kind.

dark socks, **cold** milk, **loud** noise, **wet** shoes, **happy** children

Practice/Assess Copy and distribute page 119. Help children describe the picture. Review the meanings of different adjectives for what kind. (See answers on page 131.)

Transition to English

Adjectives for What Kind
Spanish adjective endings match the gender and number of the nouns they modify. Help children see that English adjectives do not have gender or plural endings. The word *new* stays the same in *a new toy, new toys, a new teacher,* and *new teachers.* Help children practice with various adjectives and nouns.

Grammar *in Action*

What Kind? Pose this riddle: *I went outside, and what did I find? I found a cat. Ask me what kind.* Sample answers: *Was it an old cat? Was it a sad cat?* Continue with other "found" items.

Adjectives and Adverbs

Number Words

Some English number words have cognates in other languages: the Spanish word for *three* is *tres*; the Russian word for *three* sounds similar to *tree*; and the Haitian Creole word for *six* is *sis* (pronounced like *cease*).

Grammar *in Action*

My Body Teach children this rhyme. Have them point to the body parts mentioned: *I have two eyes. I have one nose. I have two arms. I have ten toes. I have five fingers on each hand. I have two legs so I can stand.* Say other parts of the body that fit the rhyme.

Adjectives That Compare

Many languages do not use comparative endings. Children may need extra practice with *-er* and *-est* endings. In Spanish, Korean, and Hmong, comparisons are made with phrases, similar to *more sad*. If children use *more happy* or *most old*, help them learn *happier, happiest, older,* and *oldest.*

Grammar *in Action*

Classroom Comparisons Have pairs of children find pairs or sets of objects in the classroom to compare. For example, one eraser might be smaller than another, while one book might be the heaviest of three. Have children present their findings.

Adjectives for How Many

Introduce Present two groups of children, one with two boys and one with three girls. Say: *Here are two boys. Here are three girls. There are five children.* Explain: Two, three, *and* five *are number words. They can tell how many people, places, animals, or things.*

Teach Present the concept and provide examples:
• Some adjectives tell how many.

three monkeys, **four** schools, **one** child, **two** feet, **five** fingers

Practice/Assess Copy and distribute page 120. Review numbers one through ten. (See answers on page 131.)

Adjectives That Compare

Introduce Draw two long lines of different lengths on the board. Point to the shorter line and say: *This line is long.* Point to the longer line and say: *This line is longer.* Write *long* and *long**er**.* Say: *You know that* long *is an adjective for size.* Longer *compares the two lines. Most adjectives that we can use to compare end in* -er: *longer, shorter, happier.* Draw a longer line. Say: *This line is the longest.* Write *long**est**.* Say: Longest *compares all three lines.*

Teach Present the concept and provide examples:
• Add *-er* to most adjectives when you compare two persons, places, animals, or things.
• Add *-est* to most adjectives when you compare three or more persons, places, or things.

A dog is <u>smaller</u> than a cow.
If you see a cow, a dog, and a frog, the frog is the <u>smallest</u> of the three.

Practice/Assess Copy and distribute page 121. Have children read their answers aloud. (See answers on page 131.)

Adverbs

Adverbs That Tell *When* and *Where*

Introduce Say these sentences: *Yesterday we came to school.* Ask: <u>When</u> *did we come to school? (yesterday)* Continue: *We played outside.* Ask: <u>Where</u> *did we play? (outside) The word* yesterday *tells more about the verb* came. Outside *tells more about the verb* played. Yesterday *and* outside *are called* adverbs. *Adverbs tell more about verbs.*

Teach Present the concept and provide examples:
• An adverb tells more about a verb.
• An adverb can tell *when* and *where* something happens.

When	I'm leaving <u>now</u>. I'll see you <u>soon</u>.
Where	I sleep <u>here</u>. I walk <u>outside</u>.

Practice/Assess Copy and distribute page 122. Encourage children to write other adverbs in the chart. (See answers on page 131.)

Adverbs That Tell *How*

Introduce Say and act out this chant: *Slowly I turn. Loudly I clap! Quietly I walk. Quickly I tap!* Explain: Slowly, loudly, quietly, *and* quickly *are adverbs. They tell* how *something happens.*

Teach Present the concept and provide examples:
• An adverb can tell *how* something happens.
• Many adverbs that tell *how* end in *-ly*, like *happily* and *sadly*.

The children sit <u>quietly</u> and listen <u>carefully</u>.

Practice/Assess Copy and distribute page 123. Read the sentences aloud to children. (See answers on page 131.)

Transition to English

Adverb Placement and Use
If children place adverbs in unusual positions, as in *We today sang a song*, show many examples of adverbs in English sentences. If children use adverbs as nouns *(Here is good school)* provide extra practice.

Grammar *in Action*

Say When and Where
Say sentences such as *I want to play.* Have children rephrase by adding adverbs for when and where: *I want to play later. I want to play inside.*

Transition to English

Adverbs That Tell How
Many languages do not strongly distinguish adjectives from adverbs. Children may use adjectives as adverbs: for example, *run slow* and *talk glad.* Help children recognize adverbs with *-ly* (slowly, gladly), but point out that not all *-ly* words are adverbs. (For example, *friendly* is an adjective.)

Grammar *in Action*

Walk This Way Write adverbs on slips of paper: *slowly, quickly, loudly, sleepily.* Display them. Have a volunteer choose one. Give a command, such as *Walk to the door.* The volunteer must walk in the manner of the adverb. The child who guesses the adverb takes the next turn.

© Pearson Education, Inc.

Name _____

Picturing Adjectives
Practice
- **Draw** a big tree. **Draw** red apples in it.

Assess
- **Tell** more about your tree. Use words for colors and shapes.

Adjectives for Colors and Shapes
Practice
• **Look** at the picture. **Read** the sentences.
• **Circle** each word that names a color or shape.

1. Give me some white paper, please.

2. I can draw that black dog.

3. The dog is on the round rug.

4. I will use a blue pencil.

5. I have a square eraser.

Assess

Which adjectives are the names of colors? Which adjectives tell about shapes? **Write** them here.

Colors	Shapes

Adjectives for Size
Practice
- **Look** at the pictures. **Read** the words.
- **Draw** a line from each animal to the words that tell about it.

elephant

short legs

giraffe

big ears

turtle

long neck

Assess
- **Write** or **say** a sentence about one of the animals. Use one of these words: *big, small, long,* or *short.*

Name _____

Adjectives for What Kind
Practice

- **Look** at the picture. **Read** the sentences. **Read** the words in the box.
- **Write** the adjective from the box that completes each sentence.

1. Mom tells a _____ story.

2. Mom and I will drink _____ tea with lemon.

3. Today is a _____ day.

funny	cold	hot

Assess

- **Say** what kind of clothes you like to wear on a cold day.

Name _____

Adjectives for How Many
Practice
- **Look** at the picture. **Read** the sentences.
- **Write** an adjective to complete each sentence. Use words from the box.

1. Hal has _____ basketball in his room.

2. On the wall, there are _____ pictures.

3. Hal has _____ books.

4. He has _____ cars.

one	two	three	four	five

Assess
- **Look** around your classroom. What do you see two of?

_____

Adjectives That Compare
Practice
- **Look** at the picture. **Read** the sentences.
- **Circle** the correct adjective to complete each sentence.

1. Kuni is (taller, tallest) than Nelly.

2. Lucila is the (tallest, taller) of the three girls.

3. Kuni's dress is (long, longer) than Nelly's dress.

4. Nelly's dress is the (shorter, shortest) dress of all.

Assess
- Who wears the longest dress? Who is the shortest girl?
  Write or **say** your answers.

Adverbs That Tell *When* and *Where*
Practice
- **Look** at the picture. **Read** the sentences.
- **Circle** the adverb in each sentence that tells when or where.

1. Tonight my school has Open House.

2. Look, Dad. I sit here.

3. I made this picture yesterday.

4. We play outside for recess.

Assess

Which adverbs tell when? Which tell where? **Write** them here.

When	Where

Name _____

Adverbs That Tell *How*
Practice
- **Look** at the picture. **Read** the sentences.
- **Write** the correct adverb in each sentence.

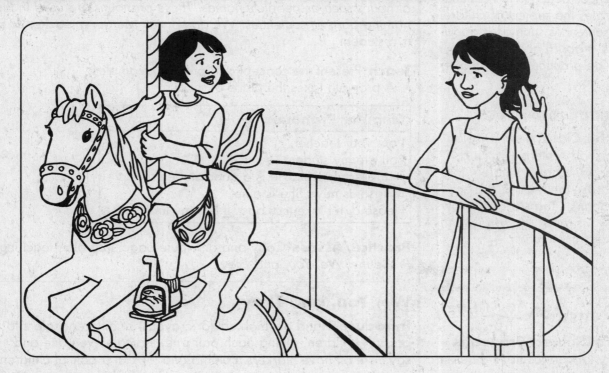

1. The music plays _____. (loudly, carefully)

2. My horse goes around _____. (loudly, slowly)

3. I ride my horse _____. (happily, angrily)

4. Mom waves _____ when she sees me.
(sadly, quietly)

Assess

Write or **say** a sentence about something that is slow. Use the word *slowly*.

Pronouns

Transition to English

Subject Pronouns

In languages such as Spanish, Chinese, Vietnamese, Korean, and Hmong, some subject pronouns can be omitted from sentences because the context indicates the subject. If children say sentences such as *Is good* (for *It is good*) and *Am tired*, provide practice using subject pronouns.

Grammar *in Action*

In the Classroom Display and read sentences such as these, and have children rephrase them using subject pronouns: <u>Ana</u> *sits in this row.* <u>Max</u> *sits here.* <u>The sandwich</u> *is the teacher's lunch.*

Transition to English

Plural Subject Pronouns

Many languages have different words to indicate *you* singular and *you* plural. Reassure children that in English, *you* can refer to one person or more than one person.

Grammar *in Action*

Noun to Pronoun Write sentences such as these on strips: *Reina, Tran, and Cali play with cars. The dog and cat run fast. Peter and you will sit.* Cut them into subject and predicate. Create strips with *We, You,* and *They.* Have children replace the noun strips with pronoun strips. Help them read the new sentences.

Pronouns

I, You, He, She, and It

Introduce Point to yourself, and say *I am a teacher.* Point to and look at a child near you, and say *You are a student.* Point to a boy and say *He is a student.* Point to a girl and say *She is a student.* Explain: *Pronouns such as* I, you, he, *and* she *are used in place of nouns such as people's names. These pronouns are used in the naming parts of sentences. We do not say* Me am a teacher *or* Him is a student.

Teach Present the concept and provide examples:
• A pronoun takes the place of a noun.

Singular Pronouns
<u>I</u> am your teacher.
<u>You</u> are my student.
Frank learns well. <u>He</u> is a good student.
Marisol is new. <u>She</u> is quiet.
Please don't take that bag. <u>It</u> has my lunch.

Practice/Assess Copy and distribute page 126 after teaching *Pronouns: We, You, and They.*

We, You, and They

Introduce Hand out markers (or crayons) of different colors to pairs of children, giving each pair one. Indicate everyone and say: *We all have markers.* Point to and look at a pair of children near you, and say, for example: *You have a blue marker.* Point to another pair and say: *They have a red marker.* Explain: *The words* we, you, *and* they *are pronouns. They tell about more than one.*

Teach Present the concept and provide examples:
• *We, you,* and *they* tell about more than one.

Plural Pronouns
Pat and I play outside. <u>We</u> have fun.
You and Ida take the rope. <u>You</u> can jump.
Min and Ismael have a ball. <u>They</u> play soccer.

Practice/Assess Copy and distribute page 126. Review gender and number of subject pronouns. (See answers on page 131.)

© Pearson Education, Inc.

Pronouns After Action Verbs

Me, You, Him, Her, and It

Introduce Display and read these sentences: *Give the book to me. She called you. That book belongs to her. I saw him yesterday.* Explain: *Pronouns such as* me, you, him, *and* her *are used after action verbs, or after words such as* for, at, with, *or* to. *They are used in the action parts of sentences. We do not say* Give the book to I *or* You saw he yesterday.

Teach Present the concept and provide examples:

- Different pronouns are used in the action parts of sentences, after an action verb or preposition.
- *You* is used in either part of a sentence.

Singular Pronouns
Pedro called <u>me</u>. I sang "Happy Birthday" to <u>him</u>. I will sing <u>her</u> a song. She will love <u>it</u>.

Practice/Assess Copy and distribute page 127 after teaching *Us, You, and Them.*

Us, You, and Them

Introduce Display and read these sentences: *Li and Pam sang for us. We heard them. I will sing you a song.* Explain: *The pronouns* us, them, *and* you *tell about more than one. They are used after action verbs, or after words such as* for, at, with, *or* to.

Teach Present the concept and provide examples:

- The pronouns *us, them,* and *you* are used in the action parts of sentences, after an action verb or preposition.

Plural Pronouns
Mari and I will have a race. Will you watch <u>us</u>? The chairs are in the way. Please move <u>them</u>. We will race <u>you</u> and Ben. We will run with <u>you</u>.

Practice/Assess Copy and distribute page 127. Help children describe the picture. (See answers on page 131.)

Transition to English

Object Pronouns
Spanish, Chinese, and Vietnamese speakers and other English learners may use subject pronouns as objects *(We like she; Yan saw they)* until they have enough practice in English to recognize and use pronoun forms well.

Grammar *in Action*

Finish the Sentence Pose open-ended sentences, cueing object pronoun endings by gesturing to different people in the room: *I will help...* [gesture toward a girl] Children should finish the sentence: *her.*

Transition to English

Plural Object Pronouns
Some languages distinguish the gender of *them* with two different words. Reassure children that in English, *them* is used for males, females, and things. Also, remind children that *them* does not need *-s.*

Grammar *in Action*

Rhyme Time Display *us, them,* and *you.* Have children call out pronouns to finish the rhymes: *I bring these flowers for Gina and Clem. These pretty flowers are just for _____. / My friends and I ride on the bus. Come along, and ride with _____. / My very best friends are you and Sue. I'm glad that I am friends with _____!*

Name _____

Pronouns
Practice

- **Look** at the picture. **Read** the sentences.
- **Circle** the correct pronoun to complete each sentence.

1. Serena and (I, me) are friends.

2. (Us, We) eat lunch together.

3. Today we had soup. (It, They) was very good.

4. Serena did not like the soup. (She, He) ate the sandwich.

Assess

- **Write** or **say** a sentence about the friends at lunch. Start with the pronoun *They*.

Name _____

Pronouns After Action Verbs
Practice
- **Look** at the picture. **Read** the sentences.
- **Circle** the correct pronoun to complete each sentence.

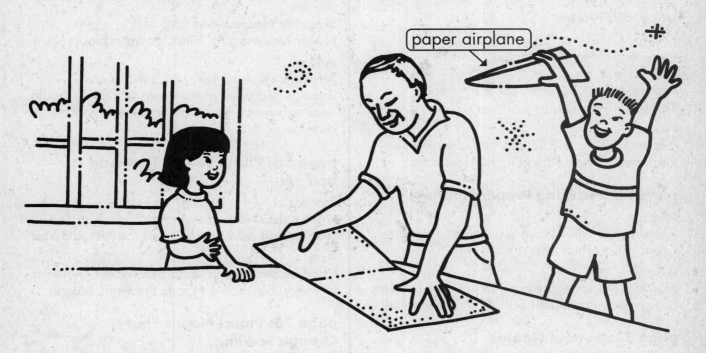

paper airplane

1. My grandfather made a paper airplane. I am holding (them, it).

2. My sister wants an airplane. He will make one for (her, him).

3. We like the airplanes. We will fly (they, them) outside.

4. Grandpa will play with (us, we).

Assess

- **Write** or **say** a sentence about the paper airplanes. Use the pronoun *them*.

page 68: Picturing Nouns

Practice
People: adults, children;
Animals: bird, dogs;
Things: ball, park, kites, table, tree

Assess
Answers will vary. Children may name any of the nouns above.

page 69: Nouns

Practice
People: boy, girl, woman, man;
Places: zoo, park;
Animals: bird, butterfly, elephant, zebra;
Things: table, sign, tree, flower

Assess
Answers will vary. Children should write or say the names of items found in the classroom.

page 70: Picturing Proper Nouns

Practice
Answers will vary. Make sure children's names begin with capital letters.

Assess
Answers will vary. Explain that the friend's name is a special name that begins with a capital letter.

page 71: Special Names

Practice
Names of People: Tom, Ann, Kim, Mrs. Garza;
Names of Animals: Buddy, Daisy, Ruby;
Names of Places: Soto Town Park, Tigers Field

Assess
Answers will vary. Children should write or say the names of specific people and places, beginning each name with a capital letter if writing.

page 72: Special Titles

Practice
1. Mr. Ed Green; **2.** Miss Ann Cho;
3. Dr. Sara Mesa; **4.** Mr. Sam Myers.

Assess
Answers will vary. Verify that children include a title such as Mr., Ms., Dr., etc., when writing each name of adults they know.

page 73: Days, Months, and Holidays

Practice
1. Memorial Day; **2.** Mother's Day;
3. Thursday, May 19; **4.** on Tuesdays

Assess
Sunday

page 74: One and More Than One

Practice
Singular Nouns: tree, sun, nest;
Plural Nouns: girls, birds, flowers, blocks

Assess
Answers will vary, but should include two singular and three plural nouns. Children should write or say the names of items found in the classroom.

page 75: Plural Nouns That Add -*s* and -*es*

Practice
Nouns that add -s: swings, clouds, hats
Nouns that add -es: benches, bushes, dresses

Assess
Children should add -*es* to *box: boxes*. Sentences will vary, but should include the word *boxes*.

page 76: Plural Nouns That Change Spelling

Practice
women, children, mice

Assess
men, women, children

page 77: Possessive Nouns

Practice
1. Pal's; **2.** dogs'; **3.** cat's; **4.** frogs'

Assess
Answers will vary. Watch for correct use of the apostrophe in written responses.

page 83: Picturing Verbs

Practice
Children should draw themselves playing and sitting.

Assess
Answers will vary, but students may use any of the action verbs they have learned.

© Pearson Education, Inc.

page 84: Action Verbs

Practice
1. sit; **2.** sing; **3.** look

Assess
Answers will vary, but children may write
sentences such as: *I eat grapes; I run;
I play a game.*

page 85: Verbs That Add -s

Practice
1. kicks; **2.** runs; **3.** stops

Assess
Answers will vary, but children may write
sentences such as *The mom claps* or
The mom sits.

page 86: Verbs That Add -s, -es

Practice
1. fixes; **2.** hugs; **3.** kisses

Assess
Answers will vary, but children may write a
sentence such as *Mom washes the doll.*

page 87: Verbs That Do Not Add -s

Practice
1. ride; **2.** run; **3.** sings; **4.** smile

Assess
Answers will vary, but children may write a
sentence such as *Mom and Dad sing the song.*

page 88: Verbs for the Past

Practice
1. visited; **2.** baked; **3.** cleaned

Assess
Answers will vary, but children may write a
sentence such as *I baked a cake.*

page 89: Verbs for the Future

Practice
Mama duck <u>will teach</u> her babies to swim. Soon,
the baby ducks <u>will grow</u> big and strong. They
<u>will swim</u> in the pond with no help.

Assess
Answers will vary, but children may write a
sentence such as *The ducks will teach their
babies to swim.*

page 90: *Am, Is, Are, Was,* and *Were*

Practice
1. *was;* **2.** *am;* **3.** *were;* **4.** *is;* **5.** *are*

Assess
Answers will vary, but children may write a
sentence such as *The girl is sick.*

page 91: Contractions With *Not*

Practice
1. *didn't;* **2.** *wasn't;* **3.** *don't*

Assess
Answers will vary, but students may write a
sentence such as *I don't like to get wet.*

page 92: More Contractions

Practice
1. *I'm;* **2.** *I'll;* **3.** *You're*

Assess
Answers will vary, but students may write a
sentence such as *He's going to play with his dad.*

page 99: Meaningful Word Groups

Practice
Children should draw a cat for the first group of
words and a cat wearing a hat or playing with
a hat for the second.

Assess
The big cat has a hat is a sentence.

**page 100: Picturing Sentences:
Naming Parts**

Practice
The sentence is about the dog.

Assess
Answers will vary; possible sentences: *The dog
runs in the park; The dog can run fast.*

**page 101: Naming Parts of Sentences
(Subjects)**

Practice
1. Mom; **2.** Ted; **3.** The pan

Assess
Answers will vary; possible sentences:
The pan is big; Ted will eat.

Answer Key

page 102: Picturing Sentences: Action Parts

Practice
sat in the sun is the action part.

Assess
Answers will vary; possible sentences:
I sat in the sun; Dad and I sat in the sun.

page 103: Action Parts of Sentences (Predicates)

Practice
1. play with my cat; **2.** barks at him;
3. runs away

Assess
Answers will vary; possible sentences:
I call my cat; I run after him.

page 104: Word Order

Practice
1. I drew a picture; **2.** This is my house;
3. My house is green and white.

Assess
Answers will vary, but make sure children start sentences with the subject or use another word order that makes sense.

page 105: Complete Sentences

Practice
1. The woman sells oranges. **2.** She cuts the oranges. **3.** You can buy honey too.

Assess
Answers will vary; possible sentences:
She sells lemons and oranges at the market; Oranges and lemons are round.

page 106: Telling Sentences

Practice
1. This is Lobo's party. **2.** We gave Lobo a new toy. **3.** We had a cake. **4.** Lobo had fun.

Assess
Answers will vary; possible statements:
We ate the cake; Lobo liked the toy.

page 107: Questions

Practice
1. Where are you? **2.** Are you here?
3. Can you run fast now?

Assess
Answers will vary; possible questions:
Can you see me? Will I find you?

page 108: Exclamations

Practice
Girl swinging would say: "I am going high!"
Girl not swinging would say: "Push me too!"
The father would say: "My arms are tired!"

Assess
Answers will vary. Encourage children to imagine themselves on a roller coaster or other fast ride. Some suggestions: *This is fun! I want more rides!*

page 109: Commands

Practice
Sentences 2 and 3 are commands.

Assess
Answers will vary, but children may write *Get bread, peanut butter, and jelly. Put peanut butter on one slice. Put jelly on the other slice. Cut the sandwich. Eat the sandwich.*

page 110: Compound Sentences and Commas

Practice
1. Dad made a birdhouse, and I will put it in the tree.
2. I got the hammer and nails, but only Dad used them.
3. Dad made the birdhouse, and now we can paint it.
4. We look all over, but we do not see the paintbrush!

Assess
Make sure children pause at each comma.

page 111: More About Commas

Practice
We took a trip on May 14, 2005. We went to Santa Barbara, California. We saw Rosa, Gus, Maria, and Eva. We came home on Sunday, May 22.

Assess
Answers will vary, but children should use a comma after each item in the series.

page 116: Picturing Adjectives

Practice
Drawings will vary, but children should draw a tree with red apples in it.

Assess
Answers will vary. Children may say their tree is tall and green. They may say the apples are round and red.

page 117: Adjectives for Colors and Shapes

Practice
1. white; 2. black; 3. round; 4. blue; 5. square

Assess
Colors: white, black, blue; Shapes: round, square

page 118: Adjectives for Size

Practice
elephant—big ears; giraffe—long neck; turtle—short legs

Assess
Answers will vary. Children may write a sentence such as *The elephant has big ears.*

page 119: Adjectives for What Kind

Practice
1. funny; 2. hot; 3. cold

Assess
Answers will vary, but children may mention warm clothing.

page 120: Adjectives for How Many

Practice
1. one; 2. three; 3. five; 4. four

Assess
Answers will vary. Verify that children use *two* as an adjective.

page 121: Adjectives That Compare

Practice
1. taller; 2. tallest; 3. longer; 4. shortest

Assess
Lucila wears the longest dress; Nelly is the shortest girl.

page 122: Adverbs That Tell *When* and *Where*

Practice
1. Tonight; 2. here; 3. yesterday; 4. outside

Assess
When: tonight, yesterday; **Where**: here, outside

page 123: Adverbs That Tell *How*

Practice
1. loudly; 2. slowly; 3. happily; 4. quietly

Assess
Answers will vary, but children may write a sentence such as *A turtle walks slowly.*

page 126: Pronouns

Practice
1. I; 2. We; 3. It; 4. She

Assess
Answers will vary, but children may write a sentence such as *They eat lunch.*

page 127: Pronouns After Action Verbs

Practice
1. it; 2. her; 3. them; 4. us

Assess
Answers will vary, but children may write or say a sentence such as *The children fly them.*

© Pearson Education, Inc.

Part 3
Phonics Instruction for English Language Learners

Contents

Introduction to the Phonics Transition Lessons

Phonological and phonemic awareness, phonics, and word study are critical components of literacy instruction for English language learners. The core lessons in *Scott Foresman Reading Street* provide the explicit, systematic instruction that all children need to become fluent readers and writers. The following Phonics Transition Lessons and Practice Pages will supplement the core instruction with customized lessons that meet the particular needs of English language learners. Lessons and Practice Pages are divided into three sections:

- **Phonological Awareness and Concepts of Print** English learners may not have learned to distinguish word boundaries, syllables, rhymes, or phonemes within words in English, or even in their home languages. Some children also may be unfamiliar with English print conventions such as the alphabet and left-to-right directionality. This section provides activities that can be used at any time to develop phonological awareness and concepts of print.

- **Problem Sounds in English** These lessons cover the phonemes that are typically the most challenging for English language learners, such as easily confused consonants and short vowel sounds. In some cases, a Model Lesson is provided along with notes for using the same lesson format with related phonics skills. Lessons in this section include Pronunciation Tips that teachers can use to help children produce the target phonemes. A Practice Page for every lesson provides strong visual support for instruction and offers additional practice.

- **Word Study** An understanding of word parts and word origins is a powerful tool for English language learners. The Word Study Lessons reinforce the core instruction and include suggestions for making connections with the home language. The Practice Pages provide visual support and context for the target skills.

Throughout the Phonics Transition Lessons, a **Transition to English** feature identifies specific challenges faced by English language learners as they acquire the target skills.

In addition to the Phonics Transition Lessons and Practice Pages, you can supplement core phonics instruction with routines such as the following:

- **Strengthen oral language skills.** Allow beginning speakers to work with partners when completing phonics activities. Encourage children to talk about their work with English, and provide other oral language opportunities with the target words.

- **Teach word meanings.** Before teaching the phonics skills, introduce the target words orally to children by using them in activities such as riddle games, chants, or asking and answering questions that use the words.

- **Provide alternate instruction.** If children have limited literacy skills, use resources such as the Scott Foresman Reading Intervention program or Early Reading Intervention (ERI) to provide literacy instruction at the level where children can participate and learn.

- **Relate to the home language.** Whenever possible, help children build on what they already know by making connections between each target phonics skill and the home language. Use available resources such as bilingual staff members, bilingual dictionaries, and language Web sites to gather information about the home language.

- **Engage children as active learners.** Children who are acquiring English may have a stronger awareness of language than monolingual speakers. Build their knowledge with engaging activities that explicitly show the patterns and structures of language. Consider games such as the following.

Phonics Four

Use with page 136.

Make and distribute copies of page 136. Work with children to generate a class list of twenty or more words that reflect the target phonics skills that children have recently studied—for example, short vowel words. Write each word on a card. Have children choose sixteen words from the list and write them in random order in the squares on page 136. Help children cut out the star markers at the bottom of the page (or use other markers). Shuffle the cards, and read aloud one card at a time. Children should look for each word on their paper and cover it with a star marker. The first child to have four marked words in a row (horizontally, vertically, or diagonally) calls out "Phonics Four!" Note: For children in early stages of literacy, write consonants in the squares, and have children listen for words that begin with the consonants.

Word Hunt

Use with page 137.

Choose a target phonics skill, such as "Words with long *a*" or "Words with the *-ing* ending," and write it at the top of a copy of page 137. Make and distribute copies to individuals, partners, or small groups. Have children look around the classroom and school, in books and magazines, and perhaps at home for words that have the particular phonics feature. They can list the words in the chart on page 137, and either draw or attach (with a glue stick or tape) pictures that illustrate the words. Conclude by having children share the words they find.

Name _____

Phonics Four

- **Write** the words that your teacher gives you. Write one word in each square.
- **Listen** to the words. When you hear a word that is in a square, **cover** it with a star marker.
- When you have four covered words in a row, **say** "Phonics Four!"

- **Cut out** the star markers. **Use** them in the game.

Name _____

Word Hunt: Words with _____
- **Find** words that share a sound or a spelling pattern.
- **Write** the words. **Add** pictures that go with the words.
- **Tell** your words to a friend.

Word	Picture

Transition to English

English language learners may have difficulty noticing certain sounds of spoken English—recognizing syllable boundaries, hearing rhymes, or distinguishing phonemes. *Scott Foresman Reading Street* provides the explicit instruction in phonological and phonemic awareness that English language learners need to develop strong literacy skills. These activities will build phonemic awareness.

Phonemic Awareness Activities

Rhyme Recognition and Production Show children words that rhyme, such as *cat, hat; hill, fill;* and *sky, pie.* Talk about the rhyming sounds. Then share a short rhyming text with children, such as a nursery rhyme. Ask children to listen for words that end with the same sounds. Say the rhyme again, pausing before each rhyming word so that children can supply the word. Then say word pairs, and have children raise their hands if the words rhyme: *bat, cat; cat, car; like, bike; cold, coat.* Provide a word that is easily rhymed (such as *stop* or *bake*), and invite children to name words that rhyme with it.

Syllable Segmentation and Blending Gather pictures or objects that represent a meaningful category of words, such as animal names, fruits, or classroom items. Have children name one of the items. Repeat the word, and clap for each syllable. Invite children to do the same for the remaining items. Have children tell how many syllables each word has. Then say aloud the separate syllables of a word *(wa-ter-mel-on)*, and invite children to say the whole word.

Phoneme Isolation Gather picture cards that include some items that begin with a target sound, such as /b/. Say the sound, and have children repeat it several times. Then show the cards, name the items, and ask children whether or not each item begins with the target sound. After children are comfortable identifying initial sounds, adapt the games for identifying the final sound and then the middle sound in words.

Phoneme Blending and Segmentation Gather picture cards of one-syllable words with three or four phonemes. Tell children you will say the sounds in one of the words so that they can guess the word. For example: /p/ /e/ /n/ *(pen)*. Then show a card, name the item, and invite children to separate the word into individual sounds: *hat,* /h/ /a/ /t/.

Transition to English

Many factors can influence children's understanding of print conventions. Children may be emergent readers of non-alphabetic languages or languages with alphabets quite different from the English alphabet. Some English language learners may be familiar with reading left to right and top to bottom, as in English. Others may be accustomed to reading text from right to left or from the bottom to the top of the page. Some have little experience with printed text. For children who are unfamiliar with English print conventions, activities such as these will help develop print awareness and strengthen literacy skills.

Print Awareness Activities

Parts of a Book Show children how to hold a book, with the spine on the left and the front cover showing. Point out and explain the title, author byline, and illustrator's name. Turn to the selection pages and read a sentence or two. Discuss how the illustrations go with the text. Page through the book, and show how the narrative continues. Point to the text on each page. Then have children practice holding the book correctly, finding the title and author, turning the pages, and pointing to the text on each page.

Letters and Words Display text in a large format, such as a Big Book page. Read aloud a sentence, pointing to each word as you read. Then frame one word with your fingers and read it aloud. Explain that it is a word, and point out the spacing before and after the word. Point out the letters within the word, and count the letters. Then invite children to point to other words on the page and to count the letters within the words.

Tracking Print As you read a book aloud, put your finger on the starting point in the text on each page. Show that you read from left to right by moving your finger along lines of text. Use your finger to show how to sweep back from the end of a line to the beginning of another, and how to find the beginning of the text on the next page. Then have children use their fingers to show the correct movement as you read the text aloud again.

Writing the Alphabet Children should be introduced systematically to all the letters of the English alphabet. Children can practice writing letters, punctuation marks, and numbers, using page 140 or 141 as a handwriting guide.

The Alphabet

- **Practice** writing the letters of the alphabet.
- **Write** more of the letters on other paper.

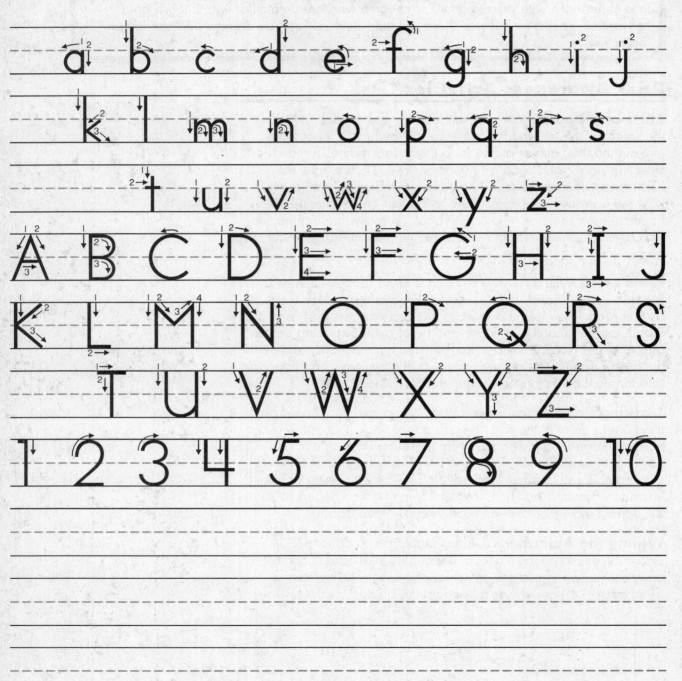

The D'Nealian™ Alphabet

- **Practice** writing the letters of the alphabet.
- **Write** more of the letters on other paper.

Transition to English

The phonemes of certain English consonants may be unfamiliar to English language learners or easily confused with other phonemes. For example, the /sh/ sound does not exist in Spanish, Chinese, and some other languages. Speakers of some Asian languages may find it hard to hear and pronounce /r/ and /l/ as separate phonemes. The following lessons provide practice with certain consonant pairs that English language learners may find troublesome. You can develop similar lessons for other consonant sounds that are difficult for your students. This model lesson gives you a pattern for teaching.

☆ Model Lesson: Words with *b* and *p*   Use with page 145.

Introduce Copy and distribute page 145. Have children point to the two items at the top of the page. Say: *I will say the names of these things. Listen to the beginning sound in each word:* bat, pin. Have students repeat the words after you. Say: *What sound do you hear at the beginning of each word?* bat, /b/, /b/; pin, /p/, /p/. *Are they the same sound?* (no)

Teach Write *bat* and *pin* on the board. Underline the *b* and the *p*. Tell children: *Let's practice saying the sounds of these letters.* Share the Pronunciation Tip.

Read the directions above Row 1 on page 145. Then say the name of each picture, clearly pronouncing the /b/ or /p/. Have children circle the correct letter for each picture. Row 1 words: *bee, pig, box, park.*

Repeat the process for Row 2, pointing out that this time they should listen for the ending sound of each word. Row 2 words: *cup, tub, web, top.*

Practice Have children look at the pictures in Row 3, say the names of the pictures, and write the words. Row 3 words: *pin, bat.*

Assess Make another copy of page 145, and cut out the pictures in each row. Group the pictures from Row 1 in one pile, and the pictures from Row 2 in another. Prepare a sheet of paper with two columns headed with the words <u>bat</u> and <u>pin</u>. Give each child the first pile of cards. Have the child say the name of the picture and place each card under the word that begins with the same sound. Then prepare a two-column chart with the headings *cub* and *cap*. Give each child the second pile of cards to sort by the ending sound.

Pronunciation Tip /b/ and /p/

When you say /b/, your lips start out together. Then they open, and a tiny puff of air comes out of your mouth. If you touch your throat, you can feel it move because your voice box is on. Try it: /b/, /b/. Now, when you say /p/, your lips start out together again. Then they open, and a puff of air comes out. But put your hand on your throat. When you say /p/, your throat doesn't move. Your voice box is off. Try it: /p/, /p/. Try both sounds: /b/ and /p/.

Adapting the ☆ **Model Lesson**

Use the lesson format above to teach other difficult consonants. The following information will help you customize each lesson. Note that Row 2 of each of the additional worksheets keeps the focus on beginning sounds rather than shifting to ending sounds, which is the focus of Row 2 of this model lesson.

Notes for Additional Lessons

Words with *b* and *v*

Use with page 146.

Teach Row 1 of page 146: *vest, bag, ball, vase* (Children will circle the correct initial letter below each picture.); Row 2: *box, vet, bus, vine* (Children will write the correct initial letter to complete the word below each picture.)

Practice Row 3: *bed, van*

Assess Create just one pile of cards for children to sort, using all the pictures in Rows 1 and 2. Use these words as column headings: <u>bed</u>, <u>van</u>.

> **Pronunciation Tip**
> **/b/ and /v/** When you say /b/, your lips start out together. Then they open and a tiny puff of air comes out of your mouth. If you touch your throat, you can feel it move because your voice box is on. Can you hold a /b/ sound? Try it: /b/, /b/, /b/. No, you can't hold it. When you say /v/, you can hold it: /vvvvv/. Your voice box is still on. Your top teeth touch your bottom lip.

Words with *c* /k/ and *g*

Use with page 147.

Teach Row 1 of page 147: *cage, game, car, goat* (Children will circle the correct initial letter below each picture.); Row 2: *cat, gull, gate, cup* (Children will write the correct initial letter to complete the word below each picture.)

Practice Row 3: *can, gas*

Assess Create just one pile of cards for children to sort, using all the pictures in Rows 1 and 2. Use these words as column headings: <u>can</u>, <u>gas</u>.

> **Pronunciation Tip**
> **c /k/ and /g/** When you say /k/, the back of your tongue is humped in the back of your mouth. Your voice box is off. Try it: /k/, /k/. When you say /g/, your tongue is in the same place. The back of your tongue is humped in the back of your mouth. But when you say /g/, your voice box is on. Feel your throat move: /g/, /g/. Try both sounds: /k/, /g/.

Words with *ch* and *sh*

Use with page 148.

Teach Row 1 of page 148: *chain, chair, shop, shoe*; Row 2: *chick, shell, chin, sheep* (Children will circle the correct initial digraph below each picture in Rows 1 and 2.)

Practice Row 3: *chin, ship*

Assess Create just one pile of cards for children to sort, using all the pictures in Rows 1 and 2. Use these words as column headings: <u>chin</u>, <u>ship</u>.

> **Pronunciation Tip**
> **/ch/ and /sh/** When you say /ch/, your lips are open and your teeth are close together. Your tongue moves as you make the sound. Can you hold a /ch/ sound? Try it: /ch/, /ch/. No, you can't hold it. When you say /sh/, your lips are also open and your teeth are close together. But your tongue doesn't move, and you can hold the sound: /shhh/. Try it: /shhh/, /shhh/.

Words with *d* and *th*

Use with page 149.

Teach Row 1 of page 149: *dad, duck, thirteen*; Row 2: *day, thumb, dig* (Children will circle the correct letter(s) for each initial sound below each picture in Rows 1 and 2.)

(continued on page 144)

> **Pronunciation Tip**
> **/d/, /TH/ (*this*), and /th/ (*thin*)** When you say /d/, the tip of your tongue touches above your top teeth. Your voice box is on

© Pearson Education, Inc.

Notes for Additional Lessons

(continued from page 143)

Practice Row 3: *dog, thirty*

Assess Create just one pile of cards for children to sort, using all the pictures in Rows 1 and 2. Use these words as column headings: *dog, thirty.*

> when you say /d/. Can you hold a /d/ sound? Try it: /d/, /d/. No, you can't hold it. When you say /TH/ in a word like this, your voice box is also on: /TH/. But your tongue is between your teeth, and you can hold the sound. Try it: /THHHHH/. When you say /th/ in a word like thin, your voice box is off, and you can hold the sound: /thhhhh/.

Words with *j* and *y*

Use with page 150.

Teach Row 1 of page 150: *yak, yell, jar, jump;* Row 2: *jam, yard, juice, yo-yo* (Children will circle the correct initial letter below each picture.)

Practice Row 3: *jet, yarn*

Assess Create just one pile of cards for children to sort, using all the pictures in Rows 1 and 2. Use these words as column headings: *jet, yarn.*

> **Pronunciation Tip**
> **/j/ and /y/** When you say /j/, your tongue is up and your lips are open. Your teeth are close together. Try it: /j/, /j/. When you say /y/, your teeth are farther apart. Your tongue is behind your lower teeth. Say /y/ and feel your tongue behind your lower teeth: /y/, /y/. Try both sounds: /j/, /y/.

Words with *l* and *r*

Use with page 151.

Teach Row 1 of page 151: *rain, lake, rope, lock* (Children will circle the correct initial letter below each picture.); Row 2: *rod, leg, rake, lid* (Children will write the correct initial letter to complete the word below each picture.)

Practice Row 3: *log, rug*

Assess Create just one pile of cards for children to sort, using all the pictures in Rows 1 and 2. Use these words as column headings: *log, rug.*

> **Pronunciation Tip**
> **/l/ and /r/** When you say /l/, the tip of your tongue touches above your top teeth and stays there. Say /l/ and feel your throat move. Your voice box is on when you say /l/. Try it: /l/, /l/. When you say /r/, your voice box is on again. The tip of your tongue goes toward the roof of your mouth, but doesn't touch it. Try it: /r/, /r/. Try both sounds: /l/, /r/.

Words with *t* and *th*

Use with page 152.

Teach Row 1 of page 152: *tie, thirty, thumb;* Row 2: *thigh, tent, toe* (Children will circle the correct letter(s) for each beginning sound below each picture in Rows 1 and 2.)

Practice Row 3: *ten, thorn*

Assess Create just one pile of cards for children to sort, using all the pictures in Rows 1 and 2. Use these words as column headings: *ten, thorn.*

> **Pronunciation Tip**
> **/t/ and /th/ (thick)** When you say /t/, the tip of your tongue touches above your top teeth. Say /t/ and feel the tip of your tongue. Can you hold the /t/ sound? Try it: /t/, /t/. No, you can't hold the sound. When you say /th/ in a word like thick, you can hold the sound: /thhhhh/. The tip of your tongue comes out between your teeth. Try it: /thhhhh/, /thhhhh/. Try both sounds: /t/, /thhhhh/.

© Pearson Education, Inc.

Name _____

Words with *b* and *p*

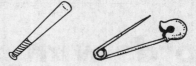

- If the word begins with the sound of *b* in *bat*, **circle** the *b*.
- If the word begins with the sound of *p* in *pin*, **circle** the *p*.

ROW 1

b p   b p   b p   b p

- If the word ends with the sound of *b* in *cub*, **circle** the *b*.
- If the word ends with the sound of *p* in *cap*, **circle** the *p*.

ROW 2

b p   b p   b p   b p

- **Look** at each picture. **Say** its name. **Write** the word.

ROW 3

_____

- - - - - - - - - - -

_____

Words with *b* and *v*

- If the word begins with the sound of *b* in *bed*, **circle** the *b*.
- If the word begins with the sound of *v* in *van*, **circle** the *v*.

ROW 1

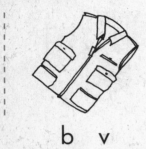      

b   v   b   v   b   v   b   v

- If the word begins with the sound of *b* in *bed*, **write** b.
- If the word begins with the sound of *v* in *van*, **write** v.

ROW 2

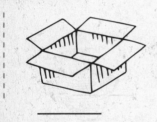         

_____ ox   _____ et   _____ us   _____ ine

- **Look** at each picture. **Say** its name. **Write** the word.

ROW 3

_____   _____

_____   _____

Name _____

Words with c /k/ and g

- If the word begins with the sound of c in *can*, **circle** the c.
- If the word begins with the sound of g in *gas*, **circle** the g.

ROW 1

c   g   c   g   c   g   c   g

ROW 2

_____ at   _____ ull   _____ ate   _____ up

- **Look** at each picture. **Say** its name. **Write** the word.

ROW 3

_____   _____

Name _____

Words with *ch* and *sh*

- If the word begins with the sound of *ch* in *chin*, **circle** the *ch*.
- If the word begins with the sound of *sh* in *ship*, **circle** the *sh*.

ROW 1

ch sh   ch sh   ch sh   ch sh

ROW 2

ch sh   ch sh   ch sh   ch sh

- **Look** at each picture. **Say** its name. **Write** the word.

ROW 3

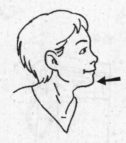 

_____   _____

- - - - - - - - - - - - - - -   - - - - - - - - - - - - - - -

_____   _____

Words with *d* and *th*

- If the word begins with the sound of *d* in *dog*, **circle** the *d*.
- If the word begins with the sound of *th* in *thirty*, **circle** the *th*.

ROW 1

d   th

d   th

d   th

ROW 2

d   th

d   th

d   th

- **Look** at each picture. **Say** its name. **Write** the beginning of the word.

ROW 3

_____ og

_____ irty

Words with *j* and *y*

- If the word begins with the sound of *j* in *jet*, **circle** the *j*.
- If the word begins with the sound of *y* in *yarn*, **circle** the *y*.

ROW 1

j   y   j   y   j   y   j   y

ROW 2

   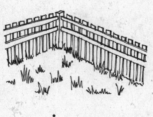      

j   y   j   y   j   y   j   y

- **Look** at each picture. **Say** its name. **Write** the first letter.

ROW 3

_____   _____

_ _ _ _ _ _   _ _ _ _ _ _

_____ et   _____ arn

Name _____

Words with *l* and *r*

- If the word begins with the sound of *l* in *log*, **circle** the *l*.
- If the word begins with the sound of *r* in *rug*, **circle** the *r*.

ROW 1

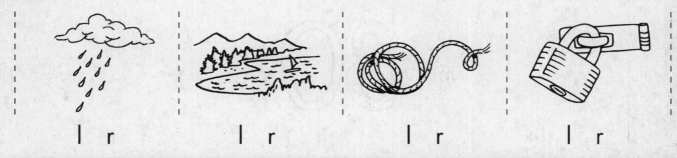

l r   l r   l r   l r

- If the word begins with the sound of *l* in *log*, **write** *l*.
- If the word begins with the sound of *r* in *rug*, **write** *r*.

ROW 2

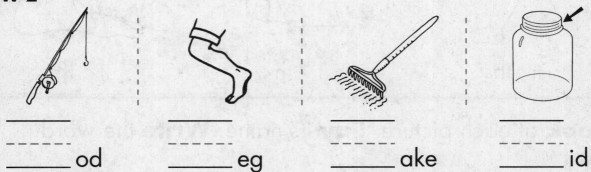

_____ od   _____ eg   _____ ake   _____ id

- **Look** at each picture. **Say** its name. **Write** the word.

ROW 3

_____   _____

© Pearson Education, Inc.

Name_____

Words with *t* and *th*

- If the word begins with the sound of *t* in *ten*, **circle** the *t*.
- If the word begins with the sound of *th* in *thorn*, **circle** the *th*.

ROW 1

t th

t th

t th

ROW 2

t th

t th

t th

- **Look** at each picture. **Say** its name. **Write** the word.

ROW 3

_____

- - - - - - - - - - -

_____

_____

- - - - - - - - - - -

_____

Transition to English

Consonant blends in English words often are challenging for English language learners because their home languages may not combine consonant phonemes in similar ways at the beginnings and ends of words. For example, Spanish speakers may add the sound /e/ at the beginning of words with *s*-blends, saying *estop, esleep,* etc. Speakers of Greek, Italian, Spanish, and other languages may not hear the distinct phonemes in final consonant blends and may omit letters when writing the words. The following lessons provide practice with consonant blends. If your children are struggling with particular blends, you can develop similar lessons targeted to those blends.

Initial Consonant Blends   Use with page 156.

Introduce Copy and distribute page 156. Have children point to the clapping hands at the top of the page. Say: *This picture shows a clap, /k/-/l/-/a/-/p/. What vowel sound is in* clap? *That's right, the short a, /a/. In the word* clap, *how many sounds do you hear before the /a/ sound? Say it with me:* clap, /k/-/l/-/a/-/p/. *That's right, this word has two sounds before the vowel: /k/-/l/. Now point to the truck. What two sounds do you hear before the vowel in* truck? *Listen:* /t/-/r/-/u/-/k/. *Yes, there are two sounds at the beginning:* /t/-/r/. *Continue with the picture for* swim.

Teach Write the word *swim* on the board. Tell children: *Usually, when two letters come before a vowel* (underline the *sw*), *we blend the sounds of the letters: /s/-/w/.../s/-/w/-/i/-/m/. Say it with me:* swim, /s/-/w/-/i/-/m/. *Repeat for* clap.

Help children to name the items in Row 1 on page 156 *(bread, flute, skirt, smile).* Repeat each name, stretching the sound of every letter so children can hear the initial blend. Then say: *I'll say each word again. Circle the letters that you blend together at the beginning of the word:* bread, flute, skirt, smile.

Practice Have children look at the pictures in Row 2 on page 156. Help them to name each picture *(block, step, frog, spot).* Have children write the initial blend to complete each name, choosing from the blends listed in the box. Then have children look at the pictures in Row 3. Help them to name each picture *(clap, crib, flag, swim).* Finally, ask them to write the names.

Assess Prepare numbered word cards, with a blend written on each side: (1) cr/cl; (2) gr/gl; (3) tr/dr; (4) sk/sp; (5) sl/sm. Give each child the cards. Have the child find the correctly numbered card, listen to the word you say, and display the correct initial blend. Words to use for each card are: (1) crab; (2) glue; (3) drip; (4) skip; (5) smell.

Pronunciation Tip
Initial consonant blends *When a word begins with two consonants like b and r, you blend the sounds of the two consonants together. In the word* bread, *take the /b/ sound and /r/ sound and put them together: /br/. Try it: /br/, /br/,* bread.

© Pearson Education, Inc.

Final Consonant Blends   Use with page 157.

Introduce Copy and distribute page 157. Have children point to the picture of the hand at the top of the page. Say: *This picture shows a hand, /h/-/a/-/n/-/d/. What vowel sound is in* hand? *That's right, the short a, /a/. In the word* hand, *how many sounds do you hear after the /a/ sound? Say it with me:* hand, */h/-/a/-/n/-/d/. That's right, this word has two sounds after the vowel: /n/-/d/. Repeat for* lamp.

Teach Write the word *hand* on the board. Tell children: *Usually, when two letters come after a vowel* (underline the *nd*), *we blend the sounds of the letters: /n/-/d/…/h/-/a/-/n/-/d/. Say it with me:* hand, */h/-/a/-/n/-/d/. Repeat for* lamp.

Help children to name the items in Row 1 on page 157 *(milk, sand, mask, nest)*. Repeat each name, stretching the sound of every letter so children can hear the final blend. Then say: *I'll say each word again. Circle the letters that you blend together at the end of the word:* milk, sand, mask, nest.

Practice Have children look at the pictures in Row 2 on page 157. Help them to name each picture *(vest, desk, jump, tent)*. Have children write the final blend to complete each name, choosing from the blends listed in the box. Then have children look at the pictures in Row 3. Help them to name each picture *(cast, belt, lamp, hand)*. Finally, ask them to write the names.

Assess Prepare numbered word cards, with a blend written on each side: (1) mp/nd; (2) nd/nk; (3) nd/st ; (4) st/ft; (5) lt/lk. Give each child the cards. Have the child find the correctly numbered card, listen to the word you say, and display the correct final blend. Words to use for each card are: (1) lump; (2) bank; (3) pond; (4) rest; (5) silk.

> **Pronunciation Tip**
> **Final consonant blends** *When a word ends with two consonants like l and k, you blend the sounds of the two consonants together. In the word* milk, *take the /l/ sound and /k/ sound and put them together: /lk/. Try it: /lk/, /lk/,* milk.

3-Letter Consonant Blends Use with page 158.

Introduce Copy and distribute page 158. Have children point to the picture of the splash at the top of the page. Say: *This picture shows a splash, /s/-/p/-/l/-/a/-/sh/. What vowel sound is in* splash? *That's right, the short a, /a/. In the word* splash, *how many sounds do you hear before the /a/ sound? Say it with me:* splash, /s/-/p/-/l/-/a/-/sh/. *That's right, this word has three sounds before the vowel: /s/-/p/-/l/.*

Teach Write the word *splash* on the board. Tell children: *Usually, when two or three letters come before a vowel* (underline the *spl*), *we blend the sounds of the letters: /s/-/p/-/l/…/s/-/p/-/l/-/a/-/sh/. Say it with me:* splash, /s/-/p/-/l/-/a/-/sh/. *Now write* stress *on the board. Ask children: What letter sounds do we blend in this word?* Underline the *str* and elicit from children the blended word: /s/-/t/-/r/-/e/-/s/.

Help children to name the items in Row 1 on page 158 *(screen, strap, string)*. Repeat each name, stretching the sound of every letter so children can hear the initial blend. Then say: *I'll say each word again. Circle the letters that you blend together at the beginning of the word:* screen, strap, string.

Practice Have children look at the pictures in Rows 2 and 3 on page 158. Help them to name each picture *(splint, spring, stripe, strong, strum, splash)*. Have children circle the word below each picture that names it. Then ask them to underline the three letters at the beginning of the word that are blended.

Assess Make another copy of page 158, and cut out the pictures for *splash, splint, strap, string, stripe,* and *strong*. Prepare a sheet of paper with two columns headed with the blends *spl* and *str*. Give each child the pile of picture cards. Have the child say the name of the pictures and place each card under the blend that begins the word.

> **Pronunciation Tip
> 3-letter blends**
> *When a word begins with three consonants like s, c, and r, you blend the sounds of the three consonants together. In the word* screen, *take the /s/ sound, the /c/ sound, and the /r/ sound and put them together: /scr/. Try it: /scr/, /scr/,* screen.

Name _____

Initial Consonant Blends

- **Listen** for the first two sounds.
- **Circle** the correct letters.

ROW 1

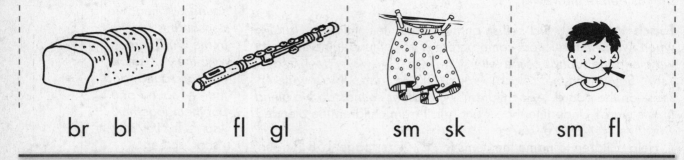

| br bl | fl gl | sm sk | sm fl |

- **Look** at each picture. **Say** its name. **Write** the letters.

| bl   fr   sp   st |
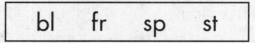

ROW 2

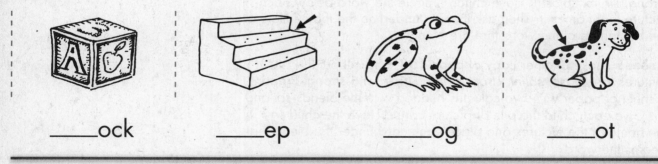

____ock   ____ep   ____og   ____ot

- **Look** at each picture. **Say** its name.
- **Write** the name of the picture.

ROW 3

_____   _____   _____   _____

_____   _____   _____   _____

Name _____

Final Consonant Blends

- **Listen** for the last two sounds.
- **Circle** the correct letters.

ROW 1

lk   lt   mp   nd   sk   nd   lp   st

- **Look** at each picture. **Say** its name. **Write** the letters.

| mp | nt | sk | st |

ROW 2

ve____   de____   ju____   te____

- **Look** at each picture. **Say** its name.
- **Write** the name of the picture.

ROW 3

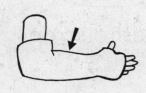         

_____ _____ _____ _____

3-Letter Consonant Blends

- **Listen** for the first three sounds.
- **Circle** the correct letters.

ROW 1

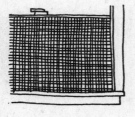      

scr   spl   spl   str   str   spr

- **Look** at each picture. **Say** its name.
- **Circle** the word that names each picture. **Underline** the blended letters.

ROW 2

splint   strip   scrap   spring   stripe   sports

ROW 3

   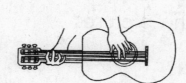   

strong   strand   splat   strum   splash   scrap

Transition to English

> Short vowel sounds may be challenging for many English language learners because they are unfamiliar sounds. They do not have exact equivalents in languages such as Spanish, Chinese, Hmong, and others. Children may confuse short vowel sounds such as /e/ and /i/ when reading, speaking, and writing in English. The following lessons provide practice for hearing and producing short vowel sounds. The Model Lesson gives you a pattern for teaching.

☆ Model Lesson: Short *a*   Use with page 161.

Introduce Copy and distribute page 161. Have children point to the apple at the top of the page. Say: *This is an apple. Apple begins with /a/. Say it with me: /a/, /a/, /a/, apple.*

Teach Tell children: *The /a/ sound is one sound of the letter* a. *We call this sound the short* a. *Repeat these /a/ words after me:* cap, am, mat, pan.

Help children name the items in Row 1 on page 161 *(fan, mop, hat, ant)*. Repeat each name, clearly pronouncing the vowel in each word. Then say: *I'll say these words again. If you hear the /a/ sound, circle the picture:* fan, mop, hat, ant. Children should circle the *fan, hat,* and *ant* pictures—but not the *mop.*

Practice Have children look at the pictures in Row 2 on page 161. Help them read the words below each picture. Have them circle the word that names each picture *(pan, rag, cat, cap)*. Then have them look at the pictures in Row 3, say the name of each picture, and write the names *(fan, can, bat, ant)*.

Assess Tell children: *I will say some word pairs. Raise your hand when you hear the /a/ sound:* pat, pet; hot, hat; bad, bed; man, main; rug, rag. Then have children repeat the word pairs after you, striving for the correct pronunciation of /a/. Keep in mind that children who have difficulty pronouncing /a/ may still be able to comprehend short /a/ words that they hear or read.

> **Pronunciation Tip**
> **short *a*** *When you say /a/, your jaw and tongue are down. Say /a/ and feel your jaw and tongue go down.*

Adapting the ☆ **Model Lesson**

Use the same lesson format above to teach the short vowels /e/, /i/, /o/, and /u/. The following information will help you to customize each lesson.

Short Vowels

Notes for Additional Lessons

Short *e*
Use with page 162.

Teach Use these /e/ words: *fed, hen, leg, set.* Row 1 of page 162: *egg, pen, bed, cake* (Children will circle *egg, pen, bed.*)

Practice Row 2: *ten, step, men, vest;* Row 3: *pen, net, leg, bed*

Assess Use these word pairs: *set, sat; tin, ten; net, not; sell, sale.*

> **Pronunciation Tip**
> **short e** *When you say /e/, your mouth is open. Your tongue is behind your bottom teeth. Say /e/. Did your mouth open? Say /e/ again.*

Short *i*
Use with page 163.

Teach Use these /i/ words: *rib, itch, fig, kit.* Row 1 of page 163: *bib, bat, fish, leg* (Children will circle *bib* and *fish.*)

Practice Row 2: *dig, lid, wig, sick;* Row 3: *pig, six, bib, zip*

Assess Use these word pairs: *pan, pin; sit, sat; left, lift; did, dad.*

> **Pronunciation Tip**
> **short i** *When you say /i/, your mouth is open, and your tongue is slightly lowered. Say /i/. Is your mouth open, and is your tongue slightly lowered? Practice: /i/. In Spanish, the letter i is pronounced /ē/. Point out that this letter has different sounds in English.*

Short *o*
Use with page 164.

Teach Use these /o/ words: *ox, cot, jog, pop.* Row 1 of page 164: *rock, box, cat, frog* (Children will circle *rock, box,* and *frog.*)

Practice Row 2: *pot, lock, fox, dog;* Row 3: *box, mop, log, mom*

Assess Use these word pairs: *top, tap; get, got; hat, hot; net, not.*

> **Pronunciation Tip**
> **short o** *When you say /o/, your mouth is open and your jaw drops. Put your hand under your chin and say /o/. See, your mouth opened and your jaw dropped. In Spanish, the sound of letter a is similar to /o/ in English. Examples: Mami/Mom; Papá/Papa.*

Short *u*
Use with page 165.

Teach Use these /u/ words: *up, bun, hug, jump.* Row 1 of page 165: *tub, truck, mop, drum* (Children will circle *tub, truck,* and *drum.*)

Practice Row 2: *bug, cup, duck, sub;* Row 3: *bus, sun, tub, rug*

Assess Use these word pairs: *fun, fin; bed, bud; hut, hot; dug, dig.*

> **Pronunciation Tip**
> **short u** *When you say /u/, your mouth is open, and your tongue is down. Say /u/ again. Is your mouth open? Is your tongue down?*

ELL and Transition Handbook

Name _____

Words with Short a

- **Listen** for the sound of *a* in *apple*.
- **Circle** the pictures of words that have this sound.

ROW 1

- **Look** at each picture. **Say** its name.
- **Circle** the word that names each picture.

ROW 2

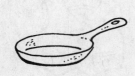   

pen	rag	cat	cape
pan	rug	cot	cap

- **Look** at each picture. **Say** its name.
- **Write** the name of the picture.

ROW 3

_____   _____   _____   _____

Words with Short e

- **Listen** for the sound of *e* in *elbow*.
- **Circle** the pictures of words that have this sound.

ROW 1

 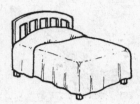 

- **Look** at each picture. **Say** its name.
- **Circle** the word that names each picture.

ROW 2

 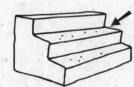  

tin   step   main   vast

ten   stop   men   vest

- **Look** at each picture. **Say** its name.
- **Write** the name of the picture.

ROW 3

 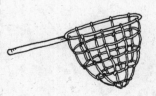 

_____ _____ _____ _____

Name _____

Words with Short *i*

- **Listen** for the sound of *i* in *inch*.
- **Circle** the pictures of words that have this sound.

ROW 1

- **Look** at each picture. **Say** its name.
- **Circle** the word that names each picture.

ROW 2

dig   led   wag   sick
dog   lid   wig   sack

- **Look** at each picture. **Say** its name.
- **Write** the name of the picture.

ROW 3

_____ _____ _____ _____

Name _____

Words with Short o

- **Listen** for the sound of o in ox.
- **Circle** the pictures of words that have this sound.

ROW 1

 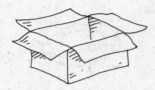 

- **Look** at each picture. **Say** its name.
- **Circle** the word that names each picture.

ROW 2

| pot | lock | fox | dig |
| pat | luck | fix | dog |

- **Look** at each picture. **Say** its name.
- **Write** the name of the picture.

ROW 3

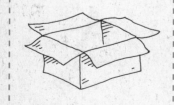   

_____ _____ _____ _____

Name _____

Words with Short *u*

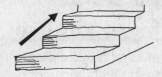

- **Listen** for the sound of *u* in *up*.
- **Circle** the pictures of words that have this sound.

ROW 1

- **Look** at each picture. **Say** its name.
- **Circle** the word that names each picture.

ROW 2

bug   cup   dock   sub
bag   cap   duck   sob

- **Look** at each picture. **Say** its name.
- **Write** the name of the picture.

ROW 3

   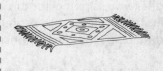

_____ _____ _____ _____

_____ _____ _____ _____

Transition to English

Long vowels and the vowel digraphs that produce long vowel sounds can be confusing for English language learners. For example, in Spanish and other languages, silent vowels are rare. Children may want to pronounce the silent *e* at the end of CVCe words, or both vowels in digraphs such as *ai* and *oa*. The following lessons provide practice for hearing, producing, and spelling long vowel sounds. This model lesson gives you a pattern for teaching.

☆ Model Lesson: Long *a*   Use with page 169.

Introduce Copy and distribute page 169. Have children point to the ape at the top of the page. Say: *This is an ape.* Ape *begins with /ā/. Say it with me: /ā/, /ā/, ape.* Repeat for *train* and *hay.* Say: *Ape, train, hay. They all have the /ā/ sound.*

Teach Tell children: *The /ā/ sound is called long a. Repeat these /ā/ words after me:* ape, train, hay, brave, main.

Help children name the items in Row 1 on page 169 *(braid, rake, apple, tray).* Repeat each name, clearly pronouncing the vowel in each word. Then say: *I'll say these words again. If you hear the /ā/ sound, circle the picture:* braid, rake, apple, tray. Children should circle the *braid, rake,* and *tray* pictures—but not the *apple.*

Point out that there are different ways of spelling long *a* words. Write a 3-column chart on the board with the headings *a_e, ai,* and *ay.* List the words *ape, train,* and *hay* in the columns where they belong. Add the long *a* words from Row 1 to the chart. Invite children to suggest other long *a* words they know that can be added to the chart.

Practice Have children look at the pictures in Row 2 on page 169. Help them read the words below each picture. Have them circle the word that names each picture. *(cane, day, rain, plane.)* Then have them look at the pictures in Row 3. Explain: *Say the name of each picture. Then write the word. Remember that the /ā/ sound can be spelled in different ways.* (Children should write *plane, rain, hay, ape.*)

Assess Tell children: *I will say some word pairs. Raise your hand when you hear the /ā/ sound:* sail, sell; back, bake; late, let; gum, game; tap, tape. Then have children repeat the word pairs after you, striving for the correct pronunciation of /ā/. Remember that difficulties with pronunciation do not necessarily indicate difficulties in comprehension.

> **Pronunciation Tip**
> **long *a*** *When you start to say /ā/, your mouth is open. Your tongue is in the middle of your mouth. To finish the sound /ā/, your tongue and your jaw move up a little. Try it: /ā/, /ā/, ape. The long a sound is similar to the Spanish digraph* ei. *Example:* rain/reina *(queen).*

Adapting the ☆ **Model Lesson**

Use the same lesson format above to teach the long vowels /ē/, /ī/, /ō/, and /ū/) and the vowel sounds of *y.* The following information will help you to customize each lesson.

Notes for Additional Lessons

Long *e*
Use with page 170.

Teach Use these /ē/ words: *eagle, feet, me, beat, we.* Row 1 of page 170: *leaf, egg, bee, pig.* (Children circle pictures for *leaf* and *bee.*) Make a 3-column chart with the headings *ea, ee,* and *e.* List the words *eagle, feet, me, leaf, bee,* and other long *e* words that children suggest.

Practice Row 2: *seal, sleep, meat, he;* Row 3: *meat, seal, feet, me.*

Assess Use these word pairs: *deep, dip; seat, sit; read, ride; mean, main; feel, fell.*

> **Pronunciation Tip**
> **long e** *When you say /ē/, your lips are stretched wide. Your mouth has a little smile when you say /ē/. Try it: /ē/, /ē/. The long e sound is similar to the sound of i in Spanish. Examples: need/nido (nest); see/sí (yes).*

Long *i*
Use with page 171.

Teach Use these /ī/ words: *ice, tie, night, sigh, pile.* Row 1 of page 171: *kite, fish, child, high.* (Children circle pictures for *kite, child,* and *high.*) Make a 4-column chart with the headings *i_e, ie, ild,* and *igh.* List the words *ice, tie, night, kite, child, high,* and other long *i* words that children suggest.

Practice Row 2: *bike, pie, light, nine;* Row 3: *child, light, tie, ice.*

Assess Use these word pairs: *mat, might; fine, fan; hid, hide; mild, made; mice, mouse.*

> **Pronunciation Tip**
> **long i** *When you start to say /ī/, your mouth is open and your jaw drops. Your tongue is down. To finish the sound /ī/, your tongue and your jaw move up. Try it: /ī/, /ī/. The long i sound is similar to the Spanish digraphs ai and ay. Examples: I/hay (there is/are); bike/baile (dance).*

Long *o*
Use with page 172.

Teach Use these /ō/ words: *rope, snow, boat, grow, sold.* Row 1 of page 172: *soap, mop, fold, bow* (Children circle pictures for *soap, fold,* and *bow.*) Make a 4-column chart with the headings *o_e, oa, old,* and *ow.* List the words *rope, snow, boat, soap, fold, blow,* and other long *o* words that children suggest.

Practice Row 2: *goat, cone, mow, gold;* Row 3: *gold, cone, snow, boat.*

Assess Use these word pairs: *coat, cot; hop, hope; crow, crew; ball, bowl; note, not.*

> **Pronunciation Tip**
> **long o** *When you say /ō/, your mouth is round. Try it: /ō/, /ō/. The long o sound is similar to the sound of o in Spanish. Example: no/no.*

© Pearson Education, Inc.

Notes for Additional Lessons

Long *u*

Use with page 173.

Teach Use these /ū/ words: *flute, moon, juice, chew, blue, cute.* Row 1 of page 173: *sun, tube, fruit, boot* (Children circle pictures for *tube, fruit, boot.*) Make a 5-column chart with the headings *u_e, ue, ui, ew,* and *oo.* List the words *flute, moon, juice, chew, blue, tube, fruit, boot,* and other long *u* words that children suggest.

Practice Row 2: *suit, pool, cube, glue;* Row 3: *glue, cube, flute, moon.*

Assess Use these word pairs: *tune, tin; foam, fume; too, toe; shut, shoot; grew, grow.*

> **Pronunciation Tip**
> **long *u*** *When you say /ū/ in a word like* rule, *your mouth is round and the opening is small. Try it: /ū/, /ū/. When you say /ū/ in a word like* use, *your lips start out in a line. Then they move into a little round circle. Try it: /ū/, /ū/. The long u sound in words like* tube *is similar to the sound of u in Spanish:* tube/tubo *(tube). The long u sound in words like* unit *is similar to the sound of iu or yu in Spanish:* unit/yugo *(yoke).*

The Vowel Sounds of *y*

Use with page 174.

Teach Use these /ī/ words: *sky, my, try.* Use these /ē/ words: *bunny, sandy, pretty.* Note that both Rows 1 and 2 are part of the "Teach" section on page 174. Row 1: *fry, bee, cry, fly.* (Children circle pictures for *fry cry,* and *fly.*) Row 2: *puppy, tie, twenty, city.* (Children circle pictures for *puppy, twenty,* and *city.*) Make a 2-column chart with the headings *y in sky* and *y in bunny.* List the words *sky, fry, cry, fly, bunny, puppy, twenty, city,* and other appropriate words that children suggest.

Practice Row 3: *twenty, fly, bunny, sky.*

Assess Use these word pairs for /ī/: *shy, she; by, bay; fly, flee.* Use these word pairs for /ē/: *sandy, Sunday; silly, sigh; buddy, buy.*

> **Pronunciation Tip**
> **vowel sounds of *y*** *When you say a word like* funny, *the letter y sounds like a long e. To say it, your lips are stretched wide and your mouth has a little smile. Try it: /ē/, /ē/,* funny. *When you say a word like* by, *the letter y sounds like a long i. To say it, your mouth opens and your jaw drops. Then your jaw and tongue move up. Try it: /ī/, /ī/,* by.

Name _____

Words with Long a

- **Listen** for the sound of *a* in *ape*.
- **Circle** the pictures of words that have this sound.

ROW 1

- **Look** at each picture. **Say** its name.
- **Circle** the word that names each picture.

ROW 2

can   day   ran   plane
cane   dad   rain   plan

- **Look** at each picture. **Say** its name.
- **Write** the name of the picture.

ROW 3

_____ _____ _____ _____

- - - - - - - - - - - - - - - -

_____ _____ _____ _____

Words with Long e

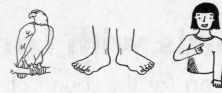

- **Listen** for the sound of *e* in *feet*.
- **Circle** the pictures of words that have this sound.

ROW 1

- **Look** at each picture. **Say** its name.
- **Circle** the word that names each picture.

ROW 2

seal   slip   meat   hay

sell   sleep   met   he

- **Look** at each picture. **Say** its name.
- **Write** the name of the picture.

ROW 3

  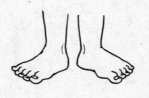 

_____   _____   _____   _____

- - - - - -   - - - - - -   - - - - - -   - - - - - -

_____   _____   _____   _____

Name _____

Words with Long *i*

- **Listen** for the sound of *i* in *tie*.
- **Circle** the pictures of words that have this sound.

ROW 1

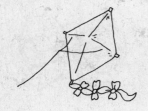   

- **Look** at each picture. **Say** its name.
- **Circle** the word that names each picture.

ROW 2

bake   pie   light   none

bike   pea   let   nine

- **Look** at each picture. **Say** its name.
- **Write** the name of the picture.

ROW 3

_____   _____   _____   _____

_ _ _ _ _ _ _ _   _ _ _ _ _ _ _ _   _ _ _ _ _ _ _ _   _ _ _ _ _ _ _ _

Name _____

Words with Long o

- **Listen** for the sound of *o* in *rope*.
- **Circle** the pictures of words that have this sound.

ROW 1

- **Look** at each picture. **Say** its name.
- **Circle** the word that names each picture.

ROW 2

got   cane   moo   gold
goat   cone   mow   good

- **Look** at each picture. **Say** its name.
- **Write** the name of the picture.

ROW 3

_____   _____   _____   _____

Name _____

Words with Long *u*

- **Listen** for the sound of *u* in *flute*.
- **Circle** the pictures of words that have this sound.

ROW 1

- **Look** at each picture. **Say** its name.
- **Circle** the word that names each picture.

ROW 2

suit   pool   cub   glee
sit   pill   cube   glue

- **Look** at each picture. **Say** its name.
- **Write** the name of the picture.

ROW 3

 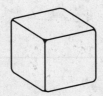  

_____ _____ _____ _____

_____ _____ _____ _____

Vowel Sounds of y

- **Listen** for the sound of *i* in *sky*.
- **Circle** the pictures of words that have this sound.

ROW 1

- **Listen** for the sound of *e* in *bunny*.
- **Circle** the pictures of words that end with this sound.

ROW 2

- **Look** at each picture. **Say** its name.
- **Write** the name of the picture.

ROW 3

_____ _____ _____ _____

© Pearson Education, Inc.

Transition to English

The /r/ sound is flapped or rolled in languages such as Spanish, Polish, Farsi, and Arabic, so speakers of these languages may have difficulty pronouncing words with *r*-controlled vowels, especially in words such as *part* and *turn*, when *r* is followed by a final consonant. The following lessons provide practice for hearing and pronouncing words with *r*-controlled vowels.

Words with *ar, are, air, or, ore*
Use with page 177.

Introduce Copy and distribute page 177. Have children point to the picture of an arm at the top of the page. Say: *This is an arm. Say the word with me:* arm. Arm *starts with the letter* a, *but the* a *doesn't make the sound* /a/ *or* /ā/, *does it?* Arm *has a different sound.* Repeat for the pictures of *fork* and *hair,* eliciting from the children that these words also have different sounds from the short or long vowel sounds.

Teach Write the words *arm, fork,* and *hair* on the board. Challenge children to find the letter that all three words have. Underline the *r* in each word as they make the discovery. Say: *A, o, and* ai *sound different when the letter* r *comes right after them. We call these sounds r-controlled. Say the words with me and listen for how the vowels sound before* r: arm, fork, hair. Refer to the Pronunciation Tip to help children say the sounds correctly.

Then help children name the pictures in Rows 1 and 2 of page 177 (*car, barn, corn, store, horn, jar, yarn, score*). Lead them to conclude that every word has an *r* after the *a* or *o*. Then ask children to draw a line from each picture in Row 1 to the picture in Row 2 with a rhyming name. Have children say the rhyming pairs aloud when they have completed the matching (*car/jar, barn/yarn, corn/horn, store/score*).

Practice Have children look at the pictures in Row 3. Help them to name the pictures (*share, hair, square, chair*). Then ask them to circle the correct word below each picture. Finally, have them write the words. You might want to write the different spellings on the board, or point them out in the title of the worksheet.

Assess Slowly say a list of words. Have children raise their hands each time they hear an *r*-controlled vowel sound. Use these words: *star, stand, stop, snore, scarf, air, apple, aim, stair, stay, horse, hose.*

> **Pronunciation Tip**
> **Words with *ar, are, air, or, ore***
> *When you say words like* far, dare, *and* more, *you make the vowel sound first. Then you bring your lips together for the* /r/ *sound. Try it:* far, dare, more.

© Pearson Education, Inc.

r-Controlled Vowels

Transition to English

Spanish does not have a sound that is equivalent to /er/, so Spanish speakers may pronounce *heard* as *heerd* or *later* as *la-tair*. The following lessons provide practice for hearing and pronouncing words with *r*-controlled vowels.

Words with *er, ir, or, ur* and *eer, ear*   **Use with page 178.**

Introduce Copy and distribute page 178. Have children point to the picture of a fern at the top of the page. Say: *This kind of plant is called a fern. Say the word with me: fern. This word has an* e *in the middle, but it doesn't make the sound /e/ or /ē/, does it? Fern has a different sound, /er/. Say it with me: /er/, /er/,* fern. Repeat for *bird* and *ear*, eliciting from the children that these words also have different sounds from the short or long vowel sounds.

Teach Tell children: *The /er/ sound is an r-controlled sound. Repeat these /er/ words after me:* fern, bird, word, hurt. Refer to the Pronunciation Tip to help children say the sounds correctly.

Help children name the pictures in Row 1 on page 177 *(purse, girl, stir, star).* Repeat each name, clearly pronouncing the r-controlled vowel sound in each word. Then say: *I'll say these words again. If you hear the /er/ sound, circle the picture:* purse, girl, stir, star. Children should circle the *purse, girl,* and *stir* pictures—but not the *star.*

Point out that there are different ways of spelling /er/ words. Write a 4-column chart on the board with the headings *er, ir, or,* and *ur.* List *fern* and *bird* in the columns where they belong. Add the /er/ words from Row 1 to the chart. Invite children to suggest other /er/ words that can be added to the chart.

Tell children: *The sound of* ea *in* ear *is also an r-controlled sound. Repeat these words after me:* ear, near, cheer, steer. Point out that there are different ways of spelling words with this sound. Write the preceding words on the board to demonstrate.

Help children name the pictures in Row 2 on page 177 *(deer, shirt, hear, tear).* Repeat each name, clearly pronouncing the r-controlled vowel sound in each word. Then say: *I'll say these words again. If you hear the sound of* ear, *circle the picture:* deer, shirt, hear, tear. Children should circle the *deer, hear* and *tear* pictures—but not the *shirt.*

Practice Have children look at the pictures in Row 3. Have them name the pictures. Then ask them to circle the correct word below each picture *(ear, deer, bird, fern).* Have them write the words.

Assess Slowly say a list of words. Have children raise their hands each time they hear an *r*-controlled vowel sound. Use these words: *germ, gel, grab, swirl, switch, ride, hurt, fear, fry, first, spun, spear.*

> **Pronunciation Tip**
> **Words with /er/ and /ēr/** *When you say words like* sir *and* word, *you put your lips close together and hold them: /er/, /er/. When you say a word like* fear, *your lips start out in a line. Then you bring your lips together for the /r/ sound. Try it: /ēr/, /ēr/,* fear.

Name _____

Words with *ar, are, air, or, ore*

- **Look** at each picture. **Say** its name.
- **Draw a line** between words that rhyme.

ROW 1

ROW 2

　　　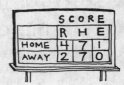

- **Look** at each picture. **Say** its name.
- **Circle** the correct word. **Write** the name of the picture.

ROW 3

　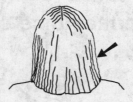　　

shape　share　　　hair　hail　　　squat　square　　　chair　chain

_____　_____　_____　_____

_____　_____　_____　_____

_____　_____　_____　_____

Name _____

Words with *er, ir, ur* and *eer, ear*

- **Listen** for the sound of *er* in *fern*.
- **Circle** the pictures of words that have this sound.

ROW 1

- **Listen** for the sound of *ear*.
- **Circle** the pictures of words that have this sound.

ROW 2

- **Look** at each picture. **Say** its name.
- **Circle** the correct word. **Write** the name of the picture.

ROW 3

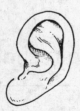

eat ear   deer deal   bird bat   fun fern

_____   _____   _____   _____

- - - - - - - - -   - - - - - - - - -   - - - - - - - - -   - - - - - - - - -

Transition to English

Inflected endings may be challenging for English language learners. For example, in Chinese, Hmong, and Korean, nouns do not have a plural form. Children may need practice adding -s and -es to show plural nouns. In languages such as Polish and Spanish, adjectives, as well as verbs and nouns, have inflected endings. The following lessons provide practice with the inflected endings of nouns and verbs in English.

Plurals -s, -es   Use with page 183.

Introduce Ask children to point to the clock in your room. Say: *Good! We only have one clock in our room.* Write the word *clock* on the board. Then ask children to point to a desk. Say: *Yes! There are many desks in our room.* Write the word *desks* on the board. Then review the two words, pointing at them and saying: *Clock, desks. We have one clock. We have many desks. What is at the end of this word* (point to *desks*) *that tells you it means more than one? Yes, it is the letter* s. (Underline the *s.*)

Teach Present the different ways to form plurals. Create a simple chart on the board with these headings and examples.

Most Words: Add -s	Words That End in *s, sh, ch, x,* or *z*: Add -es	Words That End in *y*: Change the *y* to *i*; Add -es
book → book<u>s</u> pencil → pencil<u>s</u> marker → marker<u>s</u>	fox → fox<u>es</u> class → class<u>es</u> wish → wish<u>es</u>	bunny → bunn<u>ies</u> city → cit<u>ies</u> story → stor<u>ies</u>

Point to the chart and talk about each column. Say: *Most of the time, we just add an s, like* book/books. *Sometimes, though, we have to look for certain letters at the end of a word. Say the letters with me.* (Point to *s, sh, ch, x,* and *z* in the heading of the second column.) *When we see these letters, we add -es. This word,* fox, *ends with x. So, we add -es. We also have to look for a y at the end of a word. When we see that, we make a change. We change the* y *to an* i, *then add -es. See,* bunny *becomes* bunnies.

Practice Copy and distribute page 183. Model how the first three items were completed, using a think-aloud strategy, such as: *Find number 1. The word is* dress. *How do I write the word that names more than one* dress? *First, I look at the ending.* Dress *ends in s. That's why the check mark is there. What do I do when a word ends in s? Yes, I add -es. That's why that check mark is there. Now I can write the word.* Have children complete the page by following the steps to figure out each plural form. (See answers on page 203.)

Assess Write these words on self-stick notes: *fox, puppy, brush, cap, sky, pin, bunch, girl.* Have each child place the words in the correct column of the chart on the board. Challenge them to then write or spell aloud the plural forms.

Inflected Endings

Possessives Use with page 184.

Introduce Call one boy and one girl to stand next to you. Hand the boy a pen. Say: *This is the boy's pen.* Write *boy's* on the board. Hand the girl a pen, saying: *This is the girl's pen.* Write *girl's* on the board. Then divide the class into boys and girls, and have them stand on different sides of the room. Motion to the boys' side of the room and say: *This is the boys' side of the room.* Motion to the girls' side and say: *This is the girls' side of the room.* Write *boys'* and *girls'* on the board, under *boy's* and *girl's.* Circle all of the apostrophes in the words and say: *Today we will learn what these mean.* Invite the children to return to their seats.

Teach You will be teaching children about singular and plural possessives. Use a simple T-chart on the board:

One Has or Owns It: 's	More Than One Has or Owns It: s'
boy's girl's	boys' girls'

Refer to the apostrophes you have circled in the words on the board. Say: *These are called apostrophes. They can tell you that someone has or owns something. When I gave the pen to [boy student's name], it was his pen. It was the boy's pen. He is only one boy, so I added 's to the word* boy. (Point to the word *boy's.*) *Boys, when you were standing over there, that part of the room was yours. It was the boys' side. You are many boys, so I just added an apostrophe to the word* boys. (Point to the word *boys'.*) Show the children the chart, and write the words in the correct columns. Repeat for *girls'/girl's.* Ask children to suggest additional examples.

Practice Copy and distribute page 184. Have children cut apart the word strips at the bottom of the page. Tell them that each strip matches one of the pictures. Children should match the possessive forms to pictures showing one or more than one animal, then paste or tape the strips in place. (See answers on page 203.)

Assess Make an extra copy of page 184 and cut out the pictures. Make word cards: *'s, s', cat, goat, dog.* Show the children a picture and have them select the two word cards that form the proper possessive.

Verb Endings
-s, -ed, -ing

Use with page 185.

Introduce Write the word *ask* on the board. Say: *I like it when you ask me questions. It means you want to learn. Remember yesterday when [name of student] asked me about [topic]?* Write the word *asked* above *ask* on the board. Say: *This class asks lots of good questions.* Write *asks* beside *ask. I'm surprised that you are not asking me about why I'm writing these words on the board.* Write *asking* beside *asks.*

Teach Draw a simple table around the words you have written on the board, adding headings as shown below.

PAST	asked		
NOW	ask	asks	is/are asking

Point to *ask* and say: *We change this word by adding endings to it.* Underline the *-ed* in *asked. This ending says the action already happened.* Underline the *-s* in *asks. This ending says someone is doing the action now.* Underline the *-ing* in *asking. We use this ending with the word* is *or* are. *Let's add another word to the chart:* jump. Work with children to fill in the verb forms for *jump.* Ask children to suggest additional examples.

Practice Copy and distribute page 185. Read the words *Yesterday* and *Today* and talk about how item number 1 was completed. Help children identify the pictures and read the words, then have children finish the page on their own. (See answers on page 203.)

Assess Erase the words in the table on the board. Then write a base word and ask children to write in the other verb forms. Use any of these verbs: *call, rest, walk, lock, spell.*

More Verb Endings
-s, -ed, -ing
Use with page 186.

Introduce Write *I smile.* on the board. Read the sentence and smile. Find a child who is smiling back at you. Say and write *[Name of student] smiles.* Below that, write *We are smiling.* Read this sentence and then end by saying and writing, *We smiled.* Underline the *-s, -ing,* and *-ed* in the words. Remind children that they know these word endings. Today they will learn about using these endings when they need to make spelling changes.

Teach You will teach the children about dropping the final *e* and doubling consonants before adding inflected endings. Create the chart below for display. Leave space for the example words (*smile* and *shop*), which you will fill in as you teach.

	Add -s	**Add -ed**	**Add -ing**
Word ends with e smile	✓ smiles	Drop the *e.* smiled	Drop the *e.* smiling
Short vowel, ends with consonant shop	✓ shops	Double the consonant. shopped	Double the consonant. shopping

Refer back to the sentences you wrote on the board. Circle the *e* in *smile.* Say: *This word ends in* e. *The* e *is dropped when you add* -ed *or* -ing. Write *smile* in all four places on the chart. Then talk about adding the endings. *I want to add* -s. *The check mark means I can just add it without changing anything. I want to add* -ed. *The rule is to drop the* e. Erase the *e* in *smile,* then add the ending. Repeat to record *smiling* on the chart. Follow the same teaching pattern for the word *shop.*

Practice Copy and distribute page 186. Read the words *Yesterday* and *Today* and talk about how item number 1 was completed. Help children identify the pictures and read the words. Leave the chart on display as children write the correct verb forms to complete the page. (See answers on page 203.)

Assess Erase the example words in the chart you used for teaching. Then write a base word and ask children to write in the other verb forms. Use any of these verbs: *sip, wag, hum, shine, name, use.*

Plurals -s, -es

STEP 1 **Look** at the word for one.	STEP 2 **Look** at how the word ends.						STEP 3 **Think** about what to add.		STEP 4 **Write** the word for more than one.
	-s	-sh	-ch	-x	-z	-y	-s -es	y to i, then -es	
dress	✓							✓	dresses
slide							✓		slides
baby					✓			✓	babies
box									
fly									
can									

© Pearson Education, Inc.

Possessives

- **Cut out** the words.
- **Match** the words and pictures.

| dog's bone | dogs' porch | goats' hill |
| goat's can | cat's toy | cats' plate |

Name _____

Verb Endings *-s, -ed, -ing*

- **Look** at the pictures.
- **Read** the words.
- **Add** the correct endings. **Write** the new words.

Yesterday	**Today**

He <u>played</u>.

Dan <u>plays</u>.
He is <u>playing</u>.

play

_____

_____

She _____.

Sue _____.

help

She is _____.

_____

_____

He _____.

Brad _____.

paint

He is _____.

_____

_____

They _____.

Maria _____.

talk

Sam _____.

_____

They are _____.

More Verb Endings -s, -ed, -ing

- **Look** at the pictures.
- **Read** the words.
- **Add** the correct endings. **Write** the new words.

	Yesterday	**Today**

nap

She <u>napped</u>.

Fran <u>naps</u>.
She is <u>napping</u>.

grin

He _____.

Chad _____.

He is _____.

mope

They _____.

Jack _____.

Ann _____.

They are _____.

race

They _____.

Barb _____.

Tia _____.

They are _____.

Transition to English

Compound words exist in many languages, including Spanish, Vietnamese, Haitian Creole, German, and Russian. Children may readily understand the concept of compound words but may need additional help with decoding to break English compound words into their parts. Some languages, such as the Romance languages, include **contractions**, but English language learners may need help recognizing them in English and using apostrophes correctly. **Cognates** are words that share origins and appear in similar forms in different languages. For example, the English word *lion* has Greek and Latin origins and has similar forms in other languages: *leon* (Spanish), *lion* (French), and *lew* (Polish). For speakers of languages that share word origins with English, the study of cognates can be a powerful vocabulary-building tool. The following lessons provide practice with compound words, contractions, and cognates.

Compound Words   Use with page 190.

Introduce Write the word *sun* on the board, and draw a picture of the Sun above it. Say: *The word* sun *is found in many longer words, like* sunshine. Write *shine* after *sun*. Then write *sun* again, and elicit from children other compound words that start with *sun* (examples: *sunrise, sunset, sunlight, sunburn, sundown, sunblock*). Write each word on the board. Underline *sun* in each one and read the words together.

Teach Tell children that you have been writing compound words. Write information about compound words as simple equations:

Compound Word = 2 words

Compound Word = 1 small word + 1 small word

backpack = back + pack

Below the right side of the last equation, write the words of several common compounds and ask children to blend the words, saying a compound word for you to write. Some words you might use are: *sand + box, snow + ball, rain + drop.*
   Some Spanish examples are *abre + latas = abrelatas; rasca + cielos = rascacielos; para + sol = parasol.*

Practice Copy and distribute page 190. Do the first example together, and then help children complete Row 1. For Row 2, help children read the words in the lists. Then tell them to choose a word from each list to write a compound word to name each picture (*bathtub, necktie, bedroom, teapot*). Help children name the pictures if necessary. (See answers on page 203.)

Assess Make two sets of word cards. Set 1: *cup, flash, team, out.* Set 2: *cake, light, work, side.* Keep them separate. Give each child the sets and ask him or her to form four compound words (*cupcake, flashlight, teamwork, outside*).

Compound Words, Contractions, and Cognates

Contractions *n't, 'll, 'm, 's* Use with page 191.

Introduce Say: *I'm so happy to be at school today! Aren't you? It's a great day. We'll have fun today!* Write *I'm, aren't, it's,* and *we'll* on the board. Say: *Some of the words I just used are called* contractions. *A contraction is one word that is made from two words put together and made shorter, such as when I say* I'm *instead of* I am.

Teach Display this chart, which shows how a contraction is formed. Talk through each row so children can actually see how four common contractions are made.

Start with two words.	Drop one or more letters.	Add ' and close up the word.
it is	it ~~is~~	it's
you will	you ~~will~~	you'll
I am	I ~~am~~	I'm
has not	has n~~o~~t	hasn't

Add a fifth row to the chart, working with the children to form *can't* from *can not.*

Spanish examples are: *a el → al* and *de el → del.* No apostrophes are used.

Practice Copy and distribute page 191. Have children draw lines to connect each contraction to the words from which it is formed. The first example has been done for them. Point out that the words in the third column will have more than one line drawn to them. At the bottom of the page, children will practice writing contractions. (See answers on page 203.)

Assess Make an extra copy of page 191. Cut off the left column, where the contractions are listed. Use this list. Point to a contraction, and have children say the two words from which it is formed.

Cognates   Use with page 192.

Introduce Ask children if anyone knows how to say the word for *animal* in another language. Write down the languages and the words they say on a chart like the one below. Point out that some of the words are a lot like *animal* in English. Tell children that when words look or sound similar and have a similar meaning in different languages, they are called *cognates.* Invite children to suggest other cognates they know in English and other languages, and, if possible, make lists of the words.

English	Spanish	Tagalog	Italian
animal	animal	hayop	animale

Use this lesson with fluent speakers of languages that have many cognates of English words, such as Spanish, Portuguese, French, and, to a lesser extent, Haitian Creole, Polish, Russian, and Tagalog (Filipino).

Teach Tell children that they can look for cognates when they read. Cognates can help them understand more words in English. Explain that when they see an English word they don't know, children should think about whether the word looks or sounds like a word in their home language. If it does, they can use clues in the other words and in the pictures to decide if it has the same meaning as the home-language word.

Point out that sometimes words in different languages are "false friends"—they look almost the same, but they don't mean the same thing. For example, the English word *trap* looks like the Spanish word *trapo*, but *trap* is really *trampa* in Spanish, and *trapo* is the Spanish word for *rag*. Ask children if they know other examples of "false friends."

Practice Copy and distribute page 192. Ask children to look at the pictures and translate the English words into a language they know. Children can say or write the words. Then have them decide whether the word pairs are cognates. Tell them: *To find out if an English word is a cognate of a word you know in another language, ask yourself:* Does this word look like a word in my language? Does it seem to have the same meaning as that word in my language? *If you can say yes to both questions, the words are cognates.*

Assess Have children say or write five examples of cognate pairs in English and their home language, and one example of "false friends."

© Pearson Education, Inc.

Name _____

Compound Words

- **Read** the compound word.
- **Find** the two small words. **Draw a line** between them.

ROW 1

inside   bedtime   homework   anyway

_____

- **Look** at each picture.
- **Write** the compound word. Use a word from List A and a word from List B.

ROW 2

_____   _____

- – – – – – – – – – – – – – –   - – – – – – – – – – – – – – –

_____   _____

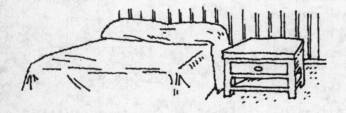

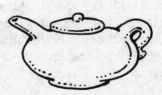

_____   _____

- – – – – – – – – – – – – – –   - – – – – – – – – – – – – – –

_____   _____

List A
neck
bed
bath
tea

List B
tub
tie
pot
room

Name _____

Contractions n't, 'll, 'm, 's

- **Read** the contraction.
- **Draw a line** from it to the correct words.

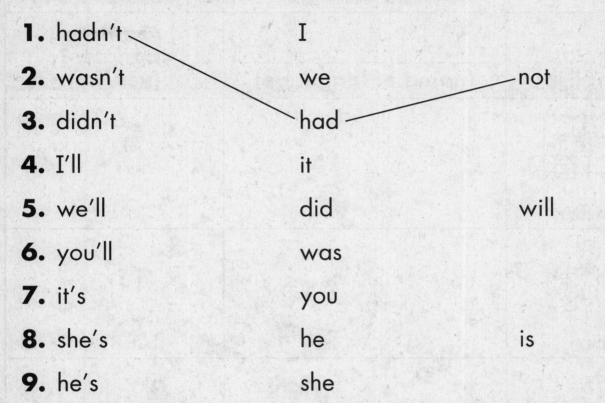

1. hadn't   I

2. wasn't   we   not

3. didn't   had

4. I'll   it

5. we'll   did   will

6. you'll   was

7. it's   you

8. she's   he   is

9. he's   she

- **Read** the words.
- **Write** a contraction.

10. I am _____

11. they will _____

12. is not _____

Cognates

- **Say** or **write** these English words in another language.
- Then tell if the two words are cognates.

English	_____ (name of language)	Are they cognates? (yes/no)
calendar		
doctor		
palace		
sandal		
train		

Transition to English

Some English prefixes and suffixes have equivalent forms in the Romance languages. For example, the prefix *im-* in English (*impossible*) corresponds to the French *im–* (*impossible*) and the Spanish *im-* (*imposible*). Students who are literate in these languages may be able to transfer their understanding of prefixes and suffixes by using parallel examples in the home language and in English. Some suggestions are provided below for Spanish. The following lessons provide additional practice with prefixes and suffixes.

Prefixes *un-* and *re-*   Use with page 197.

Introduce Take a ribbon, string, or piece of yarn, and tie a bow. Say: *I tie a bow.* Then untie it, saying, *I untie the bow.* Tie the bow again and say: *Now I retie the bow.* Write *tie, untie,* and *retie* on the board. Underline *un-* and *re-*. Repeat the tying demonstration, and elicit from the students what *untie* and *retie* mean.

Teach Present the prefixes *un-* and *re-*. Explain how they change the meaning of a word, using the chart below.

Prefix	+ Base Word	= New Word
un- (not)	fold lock wind	unfold unlock unwind
re- (again)	fold read play	refold reread replay

Explain that *un-* also can be used in words that describe feelings or ways of being. Give the examples of *unhappy, unkind,* and *unsafe.* Spanish examples include *infeliz, incompleto, recontar,* and *rehacer.*

Practice Copy and distribute page 197. The children will choose a prefix to add to the base word, and write the new word that makes sense in the blank. If necessary, read aloud the verbs and sentences, or ask for volunteers to read them. (See answers on page 203.)

Assess Create word cards with these prefixes and base words: *un-, re-, like, heat, play, use, lucky.* Have children use the cards in different combinations to make words that have prefixes. Then have children show you a base word without a prefix, add a prefix, say the new word, and tell you what it means.

© Pearson Education, Inc.

Prefixes *pre-* and *dis-*   Use with page 198.

Introduce Hold up a storybook and ask children: *What do we usually do before we read a new book? Yes, we talk about the title and the cover. We look at the pictures. We think about what the story might be like. This is called* prereading. *We do these things before we read.* Write *preread* on the board and underline *pre-*. Say: *The prefix* pre- *means "before." So, we preread before we read.*

Teach Present this chart to review *pre-* and to introduce *dis-*.

Prefix	+ Base Word	= New Word
pre- (before)	read made	preread premade
dis- (not)	like agree	dislike disagree

Point out that if children know what the base word means, they should be able to figure out what the new word means. Spanish examples include *predecir, desorden,* and *desacuerdo.*

Practice Copy and distribute page 198. At the top of the page, children circle the correct meaning for a word with a prefix that is supported by an illustration. Then, they write words with prefixes to match meanings and pictures. (See answers on page 203.)

Assess Create word cards with these prefixes and base words: *pre-, dis-, cook, made, like, trust.* Have children use the cards in different combinations to make words that have prefixes. Then have children show you a base word without a prefix, add a prefix, say the new word, and tell you what it means.

Suffixes *-ly* and *-ful*   Use with page 199.

Introduce Write *cheerful* on the board. Say the word and ask if anyone feels cheerful today. Underline *-ful* and explain that it means "full of." Say: *So, if I feel full of hope, what word could I use to say how I feel?* Write *hopeful* on the board, underlining *-ful*. Explain that *-ful* is a suffix. A suffix is added to the end of a word to change the meaning.

Teach Present this chart to review *-ful* and to introduce *-ly*.

Suffix	What it Means	Examples	Spanish
-ful	full of; tells what something is like	joyful, careful	-oso cuidadoso
-ly	tells how something is done	softly, neatly	-mente suavemente

Practice Copy and distribute page 199. Read the directions to the children, and model completing the first item. Use a think-aloud strategy, such as: *Find number 1. The picture shows a boy running. Let's read the first sentence beside the picture: "He is quick." The word* quick *is in dark type. That's the word we need to change by adding a suffix. Let's read the second sentence: "He runs ..." How can we change* quick *so that it will fit in the sentence? That's right; we need to add* -ly. *Write* quickly *in the blank.* Have children complete the page. If necessary, read aloud the sentences, or ask for volunteers to do so. (See answers on page 203.)

Assess Prepare word cards. On one side, write a base word. On the other side, write a phrase that will tell children which suffix to add. Have children read the two sides, then tell you the new word. Ideas for cards:

safe/tell how it is done (safely)   *peace/tell what it is like (peaceful)*

kind/tell how it is done (kindly)   *play/tell what it is like (playful)*

Suffixes -*less* and -*ness*   Use with page 200.

Introduce Show children the trashcan. Say: *Everything in here is useless to me. I do not use it.* Write *useless* on the board and underline *-less*. Say: *This suffix changes the base word to mean "it does not have."* So *useless* means "it does not have a use."

Teach Present this chart to review -*less* and to introduce -*ness*.

Suffix	What it Means	Examples
-less	does not have	fearless (does not have fear)
-ness	has	goodness (has good)

Practice Copy and distribute page 200. Read the directions to the children, and model completing the first item. Use a think-aloud strategy, such as: *Find number 1. The picture shows a woman awake in bed. Let's read the first sentence beside the picture: "She did not sleep last night." The word* sleep *is in dark type. That's the word we need to change by adding a suffix. Let's read the second sentence: "She was ..." How can we change* sleep *so that it will fit in the sentence? That's right; we need to add* -less. *Write* sleepless *in the blank.* Have children complete the page. If necessary, read aloud the sentences, or ask for volunteers to do so. (See answers on page 203.)

Assess Create word strips with meanings of words that have suffixes. Have children read the strips, or read the strips aloud. If you read the strips aloud, show the phrases so students can see the underlined target base words. Then have children say the word that is described. Suggested strips:

does not have <u>fear</u> (fearless)

has only <u>dark</u> (darkness)

does not make <u>sense</u> (senseless)

has <u>swift</u> speed (swiftness)

Name _____

Prefixes *un-* and *re-*
- **Look** at the pictures. **Read** the sentences.
- **Circle** a prefix. **Write** the new word.

re / un   heat

_____

We _____ the pie.

re / un   lock

_____

We _____ the door.

re / un   cap

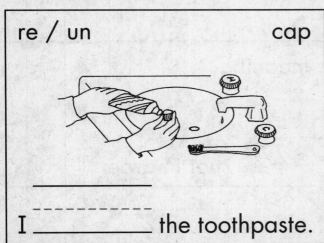

_____

I _____ the toothpaste.

re / un   use

_____

I _____ the box.

re / un   zip

_____

I _____ my jacket.

re / un   read

_____

I _____ my book.

Name _____

Prefixes *pre-* and *dis-*

- **Look** at the picture. **Read** the word.
- **Circle** the correct meaning.

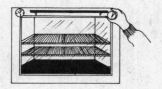

preheat

heat before
heat again
do not heat

distrust

trust before
trust again
do not trust

- **Look** at the picture. **Read** the meaning.
- **Write** the word.

not in order

_____

pay before

_____

do not like

_____

© Pearson Education, Inc.

Suffixes *-ly* and *-ful*

- **Read** the sentences. **Look** at the dark word.
- **Add** *-ly* or *-ful* to make a new word. **Write** the word.

1.  He is **quick.**

   _____

   He runs _____ .

2.  She is full of **cheer.**

   _____

   She is _____ .

3.  He is **loud.**

   _____

   He yells _____ .

4.  She is full of **grace.**

   _____

   She is _____ .

5.  He is **slow.**

   _____

   He walks _____ .

Name _____

Suffixes *-less* and *-ness*

- **Read** the sentence. **Look** at the dark word.
- **Add** *-less* or *-ness* to make a new word. **Write** the word.

1.  She did not **sleep** last night. _____

   She was _____.

2. The road has no **end.** _____

   It is _____.

3. The fig is very **sweet.** _____

   It has _____.

4.  Water has no **taste.** _____

   It is _____.

5.  I do not see a **cloud.** _____

   The sky is _____.

6.  The man seems very **sad.** _____

   His face shows _____.

Pages 142–144: Confusing Consonants Assess

b and *p*: under *bat*: bee, box; under *pin*: pig, park; under *cub*: tub, web; under *cap*: cup, top

b and *v*: under *bed*: bag, ball, box, bus; under *van*: vest, vase, vet, vine

c /k/ and *g*: under *can*: cage, car, cat, cup; under *gas*: game, goat, gull, gate

ch and *sh*: under *chin*: chain, chair, chick, cheek; under *ship*: shop, shoe, shell, sheep

d and *th*: under *dog*: dad, duck, day, dig; under *thirty*: thirteen, thumb

j and *y*: under *jet*: jar, jump, jam, juice; under *yarn*: yak, yell, yard, yo-yo

l and *r*: under *log*: lake, lock, leg, lid; under *rug*: rain, rope, rod, rake

t and *th*: under *ten*: tie, tent, toe; under *thorn*: thirty, thumb, thigh

page 145: Words with *b* and *p*
Row 1: b, p, b, p
Row 2: p, b, b, p
Row 3: pin, bat

page 146: Words with *b* and *v*
Row 1: v, b, b, v
Row 2: b, v, b, v
Row 3: bed, van

page 147: Words with *c* /k/ and *g*
Row 1: c, g, c, g
Row 2: c, g, g, c
Row 3: can, gas

page 148: Words with *ch* and *sh*
Row 1: ch, ch, sh, sh
Row 2: ch, sh, ch, sh
Row 3: chin, ship

page 149: Words with *d* and *th*
Row 1: d, d, th
Row 2: d, th, d
Row 3: d, th

page 150: Words with *j* and *y*
Row 1: y, y, j, j
Row 2: j, y, j, y
Row 3: j, y

page 151: Words with *l* and *r*
Row 1: r, l, r, l
Row 2: r, l, r, l
Row 3: log, rug

page 152: Words with *t* and *th*
Row 1: t, th, th
Row 2: th, t, t
Row 3: ten, thorn

pages 153–155: Consonant Blends Assess

Initial Consonant Blends: 1. cr; 2. gl; 3. dr; 4. sk; 5. sm

Final Consonant Blends: 1. mp; 2. nk; 3. nd; 4. st; 5. lk

3-Letter Consonant Blends: under *spl*: splash, splint; under *str*: strap, string, stripe, strong

page 156: Initial Consonant Blends
Row 1: br, fl, sk, sm
Row 2: bl, st, fr, sp
Row 3: clap, crib, flag, swim

page 157: Final Consonant Blends
Row 1: lk, nd, sk, st
Row 2: st, sk, mp, nt
Row 3: st, lt, mp, nd

page 158: 3-Letter Consonant Blends
Row 1: scr, str, str
Row 2: splint, spring, stripe
Row 3: strong, strum, splash

pages 159–160: Short Vowels Assess

Short *a*: pat, hat, bad, man, rag
Short *e*: set, ten, net, sell
Short *i*: pin, sit, lift, did
Short *o*: top, got, hot, not
Short *u*: fun, bud, hut, dug

page 161: Words with Short _a_
Row 1: fan, hat, ant
Row 2: pan, rag, cat, cap
Row 3: fan, can, bat, ant

page 162: Words with Short _e_
Row 1: egg, pen, bed
Row 2: ten, step, men, vest
Row 3: pen, net, leg, bed

page 163: Words with Short _i_
Row 1: bib, fish
Row 2: dig, lid, wig, sick
Row 3: pig, six, bib, zip

page 164: Words with Short _o_
Row 1: rock, box, frog
Row 2: pot, lock, fox, dog
Row 3: box, mop, log, mom

page 165: Words with Short _u_
Row 1: tub, truck, drum
Row 2: bug, cup, duck, sub
Row 3: bus, sun, tub, rug

pages 166–168: Long Vowels Assess
Long _a:_ sail, bake, late, game, tape
Long _e:_ deep, seat, read, mean, feel
Long _i:_ might, fine, hide, mild, mice
Long _o:_ coat, hope, crow, bowl, note
Long _u:_ tune, fume, too, shoot, grew
Vowel Sounds of _y:_ shy, by, fly, sandy, silly, buddy

page 169: Words with Long _a_
Row 1: braid, rake, tray
Row 2: cane, day, rain, plane
Row 3: plane, rain, hay, ape

page 170: Words with Long _e_
Row 1: leaf, bee
Row 2: seal, sleep, meat, he
Row 3: meat, seal, feet, me

page 171: Words with Long _i_
Row 1: kite, child, high
Row 2: bike, pie, light, nine
Row 3: child, light, tie, ice

page 172: Words with Long _o_
Row 1: soap, fold, bow
Row 2: goat, cone, mow, gold
Row 3: gold, cone, snow, boat

page 173: Words with Long _u_
Row 1: tube, fruit, boot
Row 2: suit, pool, cube, glue
Row 3: glue, cube, flute, moon

page 174: Vowel Sounds of _y_
Row 1: fry, cry, fly
Row 2: puppy, twenty, city
Row 3: twenty, fly, bunny, sky

pages 175–176: _r_-Controlled Vowels Assess
ar, are, air, or, ore: star, snore, scarf, air, stair, horse
_er, ir, or, ur,_ and _eer, ear:_ germ, swirl, hurt, first, spear

page 177: Words with _ar, are, air, or, ore_
Rows 1 and 2: car, jar; barn, yarn; corn, horn; store, score
Row 3: share, hair, square, chair

page 178: Words with _er, ir, or, ur,_ and _eer, ear_
Row 1: purse, girl, stir
Row 2: deer, hear, tear
Row 3: ear, deer, bird, fern

pages 179–182: Inflected Endings Assess

Plurals -s, -es: Add -s: cap, pin, girl; Add -es: fox, brush, bunch; Change y to i and add -es: puppy, sky

Possessives: one cat: cat's; two cats: cats'; one goat: goat's; two goats: goats'; one dog: dog's; two dogs: dogs'

Verb Endings -s, -ed, -ing: call: called, call, calls, is/are calling; rest: rested, rest, rests, is/are resting; walk: walked, walk, walks, is/are walking; lock: locked, lock, locks, is/are locking; spell: spelled, spell, spells, is/are spelling

More Verb Endings -s, -ed, -ing: sip: sips, sipped, sipping; wag: wags, wagged, wagging; hum: hums, hummed, humming; shine: shines, shined, shining; name: names, named, naming; use: uses, used, using

page 183: Plurals -s, -es

box: -x, -es, boxes; fly: -y, y to i, flies; can: -s, cans

page 184: Possessives

Row 1: dog's bone; cat's toy; goat's can
Row 2: cats' plate; dogs' porch; goats' hill

page 185: Verb Endings -s, -ed, -ing

helped, helps, helping; painted, paints, painting; talked, talks, talks, talking

page 186: More Verb Endings -s, -ed, -ing

grinned, grins, grinning; moped, mopes, mopes, moping; raced, races, races, racing

pages 187–189: Compound Words, Contractions, and Cognates, Assess

Compound Words: cupcake, flashlight, teamwork, outside

Contractions n't, 'll, 'm, 's: hadn't, had not; wasn't, was not; didn't, did not; I'll, I will; we'll, we will; you'll, you will; it's, it is; she's, she is; he's, he is

Cognates: Answers will vary.

page 190: Compound Words

Row 1: in/side; bed/time; home/work; any/way
Row 2: bathtub, necktie, bedroom, teapot

page 191: Contractions n't, 'll, 'm, 's

2. wasn't, was, not; 3. didn't, did, not; 4. I'll, I, will; 5. we'll, we, will; 6. you'll, you, will; 7. it's, it, is; 8. she's, she, is; 9. he's, he, is; 10. I'm; 11. they'll; 12. isn't

page 192: Cognates

Answers will vary. Spanish answers are: calendario, yes; doctor, yes, or médico, no; palacio, yes; sandalia, yes, or huarache, no; tren, yes

pages 193–196: Prefixes and Suffixes, Assess

Prefixes un- and re-: unlike, not like; unlucky, not lucky; reheat, heat again; replay, play again; reuse, use again

Prefixes pre- and dis-: precook, cook before; premade, made before; dislike, do not like; distrust, do not trust

Suffixes -ly and -ful: safely, peaceful, kindly, playful

Suffixes -less and -ness: fearless, darkness, senseless, swiftness

page 197: Prefixes un- and re-

reheat; unlock; uncap; reuse; unzip; reread

page 198: Prefixes pre- and dis-

heat before; do not trust
disorder; prepay; dislike

page 199: Suffixes -ly and -ful

1. quickly; 2. cheerful; 3. loudly; 4. graceful; 5. slowly

page 200: Suffixes -less and -ness

1. sleepless; 2. endless; 3. sweetness; 4. tasteless; 5. cloudless; 6. sadness

© Pearson Education, Inc.

Professional Resources

for teachers of English Language Learners

Books and Articles

Research and Practice

Antunez, Beth. "Implementing Reading First with English Language Learners." *Directions in Language and Education,* no. 15 (Spring 2002). Published by the National Clearinghouse for English Language Acquisition and Language Instruction Educational Programs.

Cary, Stephen. *Working with Second Language Learners: Answers to Teachers' Top Ten Questions.* Heinemann, 2000.

Coelho, Elizabeth. *Adding English: A Guide to Teaching in Multilingual Classrooms.* Pippin Publishing, 2004.

Cummins, Jim. *An Introductory Reader to the Writings of Jim Cummins.* Bilingual Education and Bilingualism 29. Edited by Colin Baker and Nancy H. Hornberger. Multilingual Matters LTD, 2001.

Echevarria, Jana, and Anne Graves. *Sheltered Content Instruction: Teaching English-Language Learners with Diverse Abilities,* 2d ed. Allyn & Bacon, 2003.

Echevarria, Jana, MaryEllen Vogt, and Deborah J. Short. *Making Content Comprehensible for English Learners: The SIOP Model,* 2d ed. Allyn & Bacon, 2004.

Fay, Kathleen, and Suzanne Whaley. *Becoming One Community: Reading and Writing with English Language Learners.* Stenhouse Publishers, 2004.

Fillmore, Lily Wong. "Language in Education," in *Language in the USA: Themes for the Twenty-first Century.* Edited by Edward Finegan and John R. Rickford. Cambridge University Press, 2004, pp. 339–360.

Fillmore, Lily Wong, and Catherine E. Snow. "What Teachers Need to Know About Language." Office of Educational Research and Improvement, U.S. Department of Education, 2000.

García, Georgia Earnest. "The Reading Comprehension Development and Instruction of English-Language Learners," in *Rethinking Reading Comprehension.* Edited by Anne Polselli Sweet and Catherine E. Snow. The Guilford Press, 2003.

García, Georgia Earnest. "The Selection and Use of English Texts with Young English Language Learners" in *The Texts in Elementary Classrooms.* Center for the Improvement of Early Reading Achievement (CIERA) Series. Edited by James V. Hoffman and Diane L. Schallert. Lawrence Erlbaum Associates, 2004.

Helman, Lori A. "Building on the Sound System of Spanish: Insights from the Alphabetic Spellings of English-language Learners." *The Reading Teacher,* vol. 57, no. 5 (February 2004), pp. 452–460.

Jesness, Jerry. *Teaching English Language Learners K–12: A Quick-Start Guide for the New Teacher.* Corwin Press, 2004.

Ovando, Carlos J., Virginia P. Collier, and Mary Carol Combs. *Bilingual and ESL Classrooms: Teaching in Multicultural Contexts,* 3rd ed. McGraw Hill, 2003.

Schecter, Sandra R. and Jim Cummins, editors. *Multilingual Education in Practice: Using Diversity as a Resource.* Heinemann, 2003.

Short, Deborah J., and Jana Echevarria. (2005). "Teacher Skills to Support English Language Learners." *Educational Leadership: Educating English Language Learners, 62*(4), 8-13. Available online: http://www.ahsaa.net/archives/TeacherSkills.htm

Short, Deborah J., and Jana Echevarria (1999, December). *The Sheltered Instruction Observation Protocol: A Tool for Teacher-Researcher Collaboration and Professional Development* (ERIC Digest No. EDO-FL-99-09). Washington, DC: ERIC Clearinghouse on Languages & Linguistics. (ERIC Document Reproduction Service No. ED 436 981). Available online: http://www.cal.org/resources/digest/sheltered.html

Standards and Assessment

Bielenberg, Brian, and Lily Wong Fillmore. "The English They Need for the Test." *Educational Leadership,* vol. 62, no. 4 (December 2004/January 2005), pp. 45–49.

García, Georgia Earnest. "Assessing the Literacy Development of Second-Language Students: A Focus on Authentic Assessment," in *Kids Come in All Languages: Reading Instruction for ESL Students.* Edited by Karen Spangenberg-Urbschat and Robert Pritchard. International Reading Association, 1994, pp. 180–205.

Lachat, Mary Ann. *Standards-Based Instruction and Assessment for English Language Learners.* Corwin Press, 2004.

Teachers of English to Speakers of Other Languages, Inc. (TESOL). *Pre-K–12 English Language Proficiency Standards in the Core Content Areas.* TESOL, 2006.

Valdez-Pierce, Lorraine. *Assessing English Language Learners.* National Education Association, 2003.

Language Resources

Kaufman, Dorothy and Gary Apple. *The Oxford Picture Dictionary for the Content Areas.* Oxford University Press, 2000. Offers visual support for content-area vocabulary.

Kress, Jacqueline E. *The ESL Teacher's Book of Lists.* Jossey-Bass, 1993. Provides useful word lists, including classroom vocabulary, content-area words, and cognates in Spanish, French, and German.

Longman English/Spanish-English Dictionary for Schools. Pearson Education, 2003.

Steiner, Roger, ed. *Webster's New World® International Spanish Dictionary English/Spanish Spanish/English,* 2d ed. Wiley Publishing, Inc., 2004. A comprehensive bilingual dictionary that includes technical vocabulary, idioms, and regionalisms.

Swan, Michael and Bernard Smith, eds. *Learner English,* 2d ed. Cambridge University Press, 2001. A practical reference guide to the phonics and grammar of more than 23 world languages, including Spanish, Chinese, Korean, Arabic, Polish, Russian, and Turkish.

Professional Organizations

Association for Supervision and Curriculum Development (ASCD). Periodicals include *Educational Leadership* and *Education Update.* www.ascd.org

International Reading Association (IRA). Periodicals include *The Reading Teacher, Reading Research Quarterly, Journal of Adolescent and Adult Literacy, Lectura y vida,* and *Reading Online.* www.reading.org

National Association for Bilingual Education (NABE). Publishes the *NABE News Magazine* and the *Bilingual Research Journal,* as well as the online *NABE News Digest* and *NABE News Online.* www.nabe.org

National Association for the Education of Young Children (NAEYC). Publishes the scholarly journal *Early Childhood Research Quarterly,* the practitioner-oriented journal *Young Children,* and related books, videos, brochures, and posters. www.naeyc.org

Teachers of English to Speakers of Other Languages (TESOL). Publishes the print journal *Essential Teacher* as well as *Compleat Links,* an online complement to *Essential Teacher,* and *TESOL Connections,* a periodic e-newsletter. (Also see Standards and Assessment on page 206.) www.tesol.org

Web Sites

Research and Practice

August, Diane, and Kenji Hakuta, eds. (1997). *Improving Schooling for Language Minority Children: A Research Agenda*. National Academy Press. Available: http://books.nap.edu/books/0309054974/html/index.html

Bilingual Research Journal Online. http://brj.asu.edu

Center for Applied Linguistics (CAL). Information about languages, teaching, culture, and literacy (including the National Literacy Panel). http://www.cal.org

Center for Research on Education, Diversity, and Excellence (CREDE). http://www.crede.ucsc.edu

Crandall, Joanne, Ann Jaramillo, Laurie Olsen, and Joy Kreeft Peyton. (2002). *Using Cognitive Strategies to Develop English Language and Literacy*. ERIC Clearinghouse on Languages and Linguistics. For ordering information, see Digest Series 2 at: http://www.cal.org/resources/update.html

ESCORT (formerly Eastern Stream Center on Resources and Training). Resources for use with migrant children and other English language learners. http://www.escort.org

National Clearinghouse for English Language Acquisition and Language Instruction Educational Programs (NCELA). http://www.ncela.gwu.edu

Project More. Information for K–12 mainstream and ESL teachers. http://education.uncc.edu/more/

SIOP Institute (Sheltered Instruction Observation Protocol). http://www.siopinstitute.net/index.html

Slavin, Robert E. and Alan Cheung. (2003). *Effective Reading Programs for English Language learners: A Best-Evidence Synthesis*. Center for Research on the Education of Students Placed at Risk, Johns Hopkins University. For information: www.csos.jhu.edu

Snow, Catherine E., M. Susan Burns, and Peg Griffin, eds. (1998). *Preventing Reading Difficulties in Young Children*. National Academy Press. For information: http://books.nap.edu

Thomas, Wayne P. and Virginia P. Collier. (2002). *A National Study of School Effectiveness for Language Minority Students' Long-term Academic Achievement*. Center for Research on Education, Diversity & Excellence (CREDE). Available: http://www.crede.org/research/llaa/1.1_es.html

Standards and Assessment

Center for Advanced Research on Language Acquisition (CARLA). Bibliography: Assessment of Language Minority Students' Language and Academic Proficiency. http://www.carla.umn.edu/esl/teamup/assessmentbib.html

Teaching Diverse Learners Web site, by the Northeast and Islands Regional Educational Laboratory (LAB) at Brown University. Assessment for English Language Learners. http://www.lab.brown.edu/tdl/assessment/index,shtml

TESOL. *Pre-K–12 English Language Proficiency Standards in the Core Content Areas*. http://www.tesol.org

Technology

Leloup, Jean W., and Robert Ponterio. (2000). "Enhancing Authentic Language Learning Experiences Through Internet Technology." *ERIC Digest*. Available: http://www.cal.org/resources/digest/0002enhancing.html

North Central Regional Educational Laboratory (NCREL). "Using Technology to Support Limited English-Proficient (LEP) Students' Learning Experiences." Available: http://www.ncrel.org/sdrs/areas/issues/methods/technlgy/te900.htm

Note: These Professional Resources are listed for informational purposes. Scott Foresman does not necessarily agree with the opinions expressed in the various publications, Web sites, and sources. Information about online resources and availability is subject to change.